CT/3/17

113.33.1

D1465432

ROBERT GARNIER

*and the Themes of Political Tragedy
in the Sixteenth Century*

Cur commune decus togæ & coturni
Se GARNERIVS exhibet togatum,
Nec illi suus est item cothurnus
Librum evoluc. videbis hic latentem
Suo quem ingenio sibi ipse pinxit
Grais vatibus æmulum cothurnum.
          Scævolæ Sammarthani.

Robert Garnier
and the
Themes of
Political Tragedy
in the
Sixteenth
Century

BY

GILLIAN JONDORF

Lecturer in the Department of Romance Languages
Howard University

CAMBRIDGE
AT THE UNIVERSITY PRESS
1969

PUBLISHED BY
THE SYNDICS OF THE CAMBRIDGE UNIVERSITY PRESS
Bentley House, 200 Euston Road, London, N.W.1
American Branch: 32 East 57th Street, New York, N.Y. 10022

© CAMBRIDGE UNIVERSITY PRESS 1969

Library of Congress Catalogue Card Number: 69–11027
Standard Book Number: 521 07386 3

Printed in Great Britain by
W & J Mackay & Co Ltd, Chatham, Kent

CONTENTS

Frontispiece: the portrait of Robert Garnier, engraved by an unknown artist, appeared as the frontispiece to the 1585 edition of his works and is reproduced by permission of the Trustees of the British Museum.

TO MY PARENTS

PREFACE

In the vigorous renewal of interest in French sixteenth-century literature which has taken place in recent years, surprisingly little has yet been written about the tragedy of the period, except by those whose main concern is with the theatre of a later century, and who are willing to examine sixteenth-century tragedies for their value as documents in the history of the *genre*.

This study represents an attempt to arrive at a better understanding of Garnier as a writer wholly of the sixteenth century, interesting not merely when compared to later tragedians, but for his own responses to the world in which he lived.

While preparing the doctoral thesis on which this work is based, I was supported by a State Studentship from the Ministry of Education, and also held an Old Girtonians' Scholarship awarded by the Council of Girton College, for both of which I am grateful.

I should also like to express my debt of gratitude to my two supervisors, the late Mr Donald Beves, who allowed me to use his remarkable library of sixteenth-century political works, and Dr Odette de Mourgues, who has given me constant encouragement and helpful criticism at all stages. I enjoyed useful and stimulating discussions also with Professor V.-L. Saulnier and Professor Georges Blin in Paris, with Professor Alan M. Boase in Glasgow, and with Dr Richard M. Griffiths in Cambridge.

Lastly, I thank my husband, Werner Robert, for his understanding and enlightened encouragement.

Washington, D.C.   G.J.
February 1968

ABBREVIATIONS

The editions of Garnier's plays used in this work are:

1 For *Porcie*, *Cornélie*, *Marc-Antoine* and *Hippolyte*:

Œuvres complètes (*théâtre et poésies*) *de Robert Garnier*, avec notice et notes par Lucien Pinvert. Tome premier. Paris, 1923.

(As this contains no line numbers, references to these four plays are given only by act and page number.)

2 For *La Troade* and *Antigone*:

Œuvres complètes de Robert Garnier: La Troade, Antigone, texte établi et présenté par Raymond Lebègue. Paris, 1952.

3 For *Les Juifves*, *Bradamante* and the poems:

Œuvres complètes de Robert Garnier: Les Juifves, Bradamante, Poésies diverses, texte établi et présenté par Raymond Lebègue. Paris, 1949.

These are referred to in notes as 'Pinvert', 'Lebègue I' and 'Lebègue II' respectively.

Other abbreviations used in notes and in the bibliography are:

B.H.R.	*Bibliothèque d'Humanisme et Renaissance.*
M.L.N.	*Modern Language Notes.*
M.L.R.	*Modern Language Review.*
R.E.S.	*Review of English Studies.*
R.H.L.F.	*Revue d'histoire littéraire de la France.*
R.S.H.	*Revue des sciences humaines.*

1

THE APPROACH

Robert Garnier is a writer whose reputation has suffered from the fact that the *genre* of which he was one of the earliest exponents—classical tragedy—became something very different in the hands of seventeenth-century writers; and seventeenth-century tragedy has come to be a norm by which earlier as well as later experiments are judged. His contemporaries, including Ronsard, thought him a great tragedian and ranked him with the Greeks.[1] In modern works of literary history he is almost always named as the most important sixteenth-century figure in the development of French tragedy. But Garnier's contemporaries mention the specific qualities which they admire in his work: his evocation of the supernatural and the underworld, his erudition, the pathetic quality of his plays, their relevance to contemporary troubles, the dignity and grandeur of his style.[2] Modern critics, on the other hand, seem to place him on a pedestal only to knock him down again, criticizing his plays for weakness of construction, thinness or inconsistency of character-drawing, over-indebtedness to Seneca. Often, explicitly or implicitly, the final judgment seems to be one of regret that this precursor of Corneille and Racine did not write Cornelian or Racinian tragedies. One of the extreme instances of this (but there are many others) is in the speech made at the unveiling of a bust of Garnier at his birth-place in 1934 where the speaker, the Duc de la Force, after talking about 'les vagissements de la tragédie de Garnier' and 'cet excellent devoir de rhétorique' at last finds something he can praise, in these terms: 'Ouvrons

---

[1] See *liminaires* by Robert Estienne (Pinvert, p. 12), Paschal Robin du Faux (Pinvert, p. 167), Amadis Jamyn (Pinvert, p. 93) and Ronsard (Pinvert, p. 92); also Dorat's tribute (*J. Aurati . . . Poemata*, Paris, 1586, 2e partie, p. 65).

[2] Evocation of the underworld: Flaminio de Birague (Pinvert, p. 11). Erudition: Belleau (Pinvert, p. 10). Pathos: Cl. Binet (Pinvert, pp. 11–12). Relevance: Robert Estienne (Pinvert, p. 13). Style: Ronsard (Pinvert, p. 92; Lebègue I, p. 10)

1

maintenant la *Troade* : voici un passage qui semble une variante d'*Andromaque*'.[1] When Garnier is praised, it is often rather for his lyrical powers, for the importance of his work as a stage in the history of the drama, or for the felicity of selected *beaux vers* and *sentences* than for any central qualities or merits of his theatre. As Thierry Maulnier remarks: 'L'oubli ou le mépris vaudraient mieux pour lui que la condescendance avec laquelle on lui reconnaît quelques mérites'.[2]

It may seem that a study of the political elements in Garnier's work runs the same risk of undue emphasis on a peripheral aspect; but I hope to show that the political elements are central, not accessory, to Garnier's tragedy, and an examination of these elements and of the way in which they are incorporated into the plays ought to result in a more satisfactory way of looking at each play as a whole. As a partial justification of this point of view I shall begin by examining the reasons why some of the approaches to Garnier most often used seem inadequate.

To begin with one of the more recent, there is the 'baroque' approach. Because of the failure to find a satisfactory and generally accepted definition of how the word 'baroque' is to be used in literary history or criticism, the critics who consider Garnier a baroque writer seem to have no common reason for doing so. To different people, Garnier's imagery, his descriptions of physical cruelty, his religious themes and even his use of stichomythia have appeared baroque.[3] Such an approach may be helpful and stimulating in directing our attention to certain interesting features of Garnier's style; but it seems to lead to distortion. Thus Dora Frick emphasizes some characteristics of Garnier's imagery unduly, and by her stress on images of chaos and horror she tends to cover up more 'classical' aspects of Garnier's work and also to lose sight of the possibility that the

---

[1] Duc de la Force, *Inauguration d'un buste de Robert Garnier, à La Ferté-Bernard* (*16 septembre, 1934*) (Paris, 1934), pp. 10, 14.

[2] Thierry Maulnier, *Introduction à la poésie française* (Paris, 1939) p. 82.

[3] See, e.g., Dora Frick, *Garnier als barocker Dichter* (Zurich, 1951); Philip Butler, *Classicisme et baroque dans l'œuvre de Racine* (Paris, 1959); Darnell Roaten, *Structural forms in the French theater, 1500–1700* (Philadelphia, 1960).

tragedies may embody a serious and consistent political or moral doctrine. This leads to another objection to the 'baroque' approach—that it deals almost exclusively with form and style; thus Dora Frick discusses imagery and vocabulary, Darnell Roaten the structure of the plays, but it would be interesting to hear about what Garnier is saying as well as how he says it.

Then there are critics who have appreciated Garnier for his lyrical powers.[1] I certainly do not wish to deprecate Garnier's supple use of metres, the poignant melancholy of a chorus such as 'Comme veut-on que maintenant' (*Les Juifves*, Act III), the solemn grace of the lament at the end of *Porcie*, the balanced construction and firm movement of the hunting chorus in the first act of *Hippolyte*. But if Garnier's tragedies are only worth preserving for their choruses then they fail as tragedies. Indeed, it is usual for praise of the lyrical elements in the plays to be accompanied by severe criticism of construction, handling of plot or other dramatic elements.

It seems that these criticisms of Garnier as a dramatic poet are based on criteria formed from seventeenth-century tragedy. This is clear when Emile Faguet writes: 'Ce que nous demandons, avec nos idées modernes, à une tragédie, c'est de nous montrer les forces opposées qui sont les ressorts du drame, se rencontrant, se heurtant de plein contact . . .' and quotes as examples scenes from seventeenth-century plays such as *Le Cid*, *Britannicus* and *Phèdre*.[2]

Certainly we shall not find in Garnier the tight, unilinear construction, the delicate balance between inevitability and dramatic surprise, which characterize a Racinian tragedy; but why look for them ? This tendency to regard seventeenth-century tragedy as representing some kind of 'norm' for the *genre* is probably the origin of another frequent, and equally unhelpful, approach to Garnier, that which places the plays in an order of merit based on their 'psychological' value. This leads to widely varying conclusions; thus M. S. Bernage finds that *Hippolyte* is,

[1] 'Ce sont les parties de son talent, non pas les seules recommandables, comme on l'a trop dit, mais incontestablement les plus brillantes.' Emile Faguet, *La Tragédie française au XVIe siècle (1550–1600)* (Paris, 1883) p. 255.
[2] Emile Faguet, *op. cit.*, p. 199.

with *Marc-Antoine*, 'son plus faible ouvrage' and suggests that the reason why *Marc-Antoine* is so poor lies in the character-drawing, because the character of Cléopâtre is 'trop peu conforme à l'histoire pour nous arrêter longuement'; Emile Faguet on the other hand considers *Marc-Antoine* 'la première pièce vraiment recommandable de Garnier' and praises the 'fond vrai et naturel' of Marc-Antoine's character while regretting that the character-drawing is rather swamped by rhetoric; he also comments on the psychological subtlety in the character of Phèdre in *Hippolyte*; Raymond Lebègue says that Marc-Antoine is the only character with any solidity in the Roman tragedies.[1] Yet there is nothing in the writings of sixteenth-century theorists of tragedy, nor in the prefaces of Garnier and other writers of tragedies, nor in the comments (e.g. in *liminaires*) by the contemporary admirers of these writers, to suggest that presentation of character, or psychological analysis, entered into their conception of tragedy. Thus Grévin: 'La Tragédie donc (comme dit Aristote en son art poëtique) est une imitation ou représentation de quelque faict illustre et grand de soymesme, comme est celuy touchant la mort de Jules César.'[2] Jean de la Taille: 'La vraye et seule intention d'une tragedie est d'esmouvoir et de poindre merveilleusement les affections d'un chascun.'[3] Ronsard: 'La Tragedie et Comedie, lesquelles sont du tout didascaliques et enseignantes'.[4] Garnier: 'Je sçay qu'il n'est genre de Poëmes moins agreable que cestuy-cy, qui ne represente que les malheurs lamentables des princes, avec les saccagemens des peuples'; 'les cris et les horreurs de mes Tragédies'.[5]

---

[1] M. S. Bernage, *Etude sur Robert Garnier* (Paris, 1880) p. 66, pp. 58–9; Emile Faguet, *Tragédie française*, pp. 200, 197, 190; Raymond Lebègue, *La Tragédie française de la Renaissance* (Brussels, 1944) p. 45.

[2] Jacques Grévin, *Brief discours pour l'intelligence de ce théâtre* (1561), in *Théâtre complet et poésies choisies*, ed. L. Pinvert (Paris, 1922), p. 6.

[3] Jean de la Taille, *De l'Art de la tragédie*, ed. F. West (Manchester, 1939), p. 24.

[4] Pierre de Ronsard, *La Franciade* (*1572*), *deuxième partie*, in *Œuvres complètes*, ed. P. Laumonier (Paris, 1914–67), vol. XVI, part 2, p. 334. (This phrase is in the 1587 preface to the *Franciade*, prepared for publication by Cl. Binet after Ronsard's death).

[5] Robert Garnier, dedicatory letters of *La Troade* (Lebègue I, p. 9) and *Cornélie* (Pinvert, p. 90).

Robert Estienne :

> France, appren par ces vers, que ton Garnier t'adresse,
> Appren ce que tu dois pour ton bien éviter;
> Que les malheurs d'autruy te puissent profiter,
> Et sois sage aux despens de Rome et de la Grèce.[1]

The elements of sixteenth-century tragedy suggested by these statements are a dignified subject easily lending itself to political treatment ('la mort de Jules César', 'les malheurs lamentables des princes, avec les saccagemens des peuples'), an element of pathos and a didactic intention. A comparison of Garnier's prefaces, where he emphasizes the appropriateness of his themes to the troubled years of the French religious wars, with for example Racine's preface to *Phèdre*, of which the first four paragraphs are devoted to a discussion of the characters, gives a fair picture of the totally different approaches of the two writers. It seems only just not to criticize Garnier for failing to fulfil intentions which were not his. This does not mean that we cannot discuss Garnier's characters at all, nor that Garnier does not differentiate them, giving them words appropriate to the idea he intends us to form of them. But both his methods and his intentions are different from those of seventeenth-century dramatists. His characters are to some extent 'types'—the Tyrant, the Conqueror, the Good King—which means that they are without the complexity of a seventeenth-century 'individual' character.[2] Nor have they the rigorous internal logic of a Racinian character. If Garnier's Phèdre is compared to Racine's, she seems to lack consistency because her progress from one state of mind to another is not traced; we are merely presented with the succeeding attitudes as they occur. In terms of our experience of other people's feelings this may be as 'realistic' a method as Racine's; but to defend it on these grounds would be to replace one misleading approach by another. It seems truer to say that those aspects of a personality are used which are dramatically necessary. Thus Phèdre's nurse changes from strong disapproval of

---

[1] Robert Estienne, *liminaire* to Garnier's theatre (Pinvert, p. 13).

[2] See M. C. Bradbrook, *Themes and conventions of Elizabethan tragedy* (Cambridge, 1935) chapter iii ('Conventions of action'), for a full discussion of the dramatic convention of 'typical characters'.

illicit love to eager plotting on Phèdre's behalf because that is the way in which the next incident is to be brought about. One is tempted to compare this technique with that of Rabelais, whose Frère Jean, for instance, may be a good monk, a bad monk or no monk at all, according to the use Rabelais wishes to make of him at a particular moment in the story.

The 'Senecan' approach to Garnier is one which has often produced misleading judgments on his plays. Garnier's debt to Seneca has frequently been exaggerated. It is worth remembering for a start that he uses only three subjects treated by Seneca —the themes of Hippolytus, the Trojan women and Antigone. Even when he is translating or paraphrasing a specific Senecan model, he does it with more selectiveness and originality than might be supposed from the comments of some critics and editors. This is true even of *Hippolyte* which is, of all Garnier's plays, the one closest to Seneca; Lucien Pinvert says of it: 'Garnier s'est inspiré [. . .] de l'*Hippolyte* de Sénèque, qu'il suit pas à pas.'[1] Emile Faguet regards it as a translation.[2] Yet in the passage which is perhaps closest of all to Seneca, the scene of Phèdre's declaration of love to Hippolyte, there are considerable differences between the two texts. The most obvious is that Garnier's version is half as long again; the passage from 'Je prendray le soucy de vos enfans, mes frères' to 'Ayez pitié de moy' (Pinvert, pp. 292–4) is sixty-two lines long, to Seneca's forty. Garnier gives more details of description and sensation, lengthens the comparison of the burning building, fills out Seneca's over-epigrammatic style, and at the same time passes over, in the composite portrait of Theseus-Hippolytus, the *pudor* and the suggestion of arrogance which form part of Seneca's description. He improves on his model by cutting out the discursive passage in which Phaedra comments that Hippolytus resembles his mother as well as his father. He also leaves out the lines in which Phaedra protests that her life hitherto has been irreproachably pure. There are other modifications, such as the way in which Garnier changes the emphasis when translating

[1] Pinvert, p. x.
[2] Emile Faguet, *Tragédie française*, pp. 188, 256.

Seneca's

> domus sorores una corripuit duas:
> te genitor at me natus.

> (*Hippolytus, 665–6*)

This becomes in Garnier's version 'Tu as aimé le père [. . .] et moy j'aime le fils', with Phèdre as the agent, not the helpless victim. This is the play in which Garnier is following Seneca most closely, and this is the scene of that play which is nearest to Seneca, but even here Garnier makes the text his own; and the emphasis of the play as a whole is in any case changed from the start by the prologue, spoken by Egée's ghost, which directs the attention to Thésée rather than to Hippolyte or Phèdre.

In short, Garnier's 'Senecan' tragedies are far from being close reproductions of the text of Seneca. We shall examine the differences in tone and treatment more closely in the next chapter.

I have tried to show why I consider various approaches to Garnier's plays to be unsatisfactory or misleading; in the course of this study I shall put forward an approach which seems to me more satisfactory because it takes account of the period in which Garnier wrote, his own statements about his plays, and possible relationships between these plays and other, overtly political, writings of the period. I am considering Garnier as a political dramatist; that is, a dramatist who is making a statement of political views, or airing political problems in his works, and whose dramatic technique can best be understood in the light of its connection with this political content.

2

SENECA REVISITED

In the previous chapter I pointed out one defect in what I have called the Senecan approach to Garnier—that it implies a closer imitation of Senecan texts than Garnier practised and therefore overlooks some elements of Garnier's originality. But the whole question is more complicated than this and calls for detailed examination. There are really two points to be discussed: firstly, was Senecan influence on early classical tragedy in France a bad thing? secondly, what are the advantages of looking at sixteenth-century French tragedy as 'Senecan' tragedy?

THE MIXED BLESSING OF SENECA

There is a tendency among critics commenting on the great influence of Seneca on the development of French tragedy to assume that this influence was regrettable. Seneca, they seem to feel, was the worst calamity that could have happened to the promising new *genre*. If only Seneca had not been known, or at least not admired, in sixteenth-century France, if only French authors had gone straight to the Greeks, or to non-dramatic sources such as the Bible, the historians or Ariosto, then (they seem to imply) there might have been tragedies like Racine's in the sixteenth century. It hardly needs saying that this would have been impossible; but it is worth considering, in opposition to this 'might-have-been' world of sixteenth-century tragedy without Seneca, some of the positive benefits arising from the popularity of Seneca. One benefit can be seen very clearly by an analogy with Petrarch. The reason why Petrarch was so widely imitated was that so much in the *Canzoniere* was imitable. For writers trying out a new poetic language (in England, the Tudor lyricists; in France, the Pléiade) the set of easily translatable themes and images which they found in Petrarch, and even more clearly in his Italian imitators, provided convenient basic material to work on. By taking over the Petrarchan convention they simplified their task because they had not to work out their own solutions to problems about the nature of love, the relationship between lovers and so on, but could use the ready-made attitudes of Petrarch and his imitators; thus they were free to concentrate on finding solutions to equally important problems concerning form, style, sound-patterns and the manipulation of their own language. It can be seen that Seneca's plays could perform the same service for dramatists as the *Canzoniere* for lyric poets. In Senecan drama French writers found what amounted to a guide for their own experiments. They found a certain form—the use of few characters, the technique of launching the play *in medias res*, alternation of dialogue and chorus, with the chorus used to mark pauses in the action and thus to stress the shape of the play. They found conventions—some stock characters, a habit of keeping most violent action off the stage, the use of a confidant to avoid soliloquies by the leading characters, the use of dreams, of the supernatural and of dramatic irony. They found a highly sophisticated rhetorical use of language which, in spite of its sophistication, included simple, striking, easily imitable devices and effects. This is comparable to what the Pléiade poets found in Petrarchism—the sonnet form, the cycle of love poems, a set of statements about the nature of love and the attitude of the lover, and the verbal formulæ in which to frame these statements. Obviously the convention can become barren and tiresome, but it starts off fruitfully enough.

Another characteristic of Senecan drama which could lead to its influence being at least partly beneficial is its sententiousness. It may be objected that sententiousness is one of the defects of sixteenth-century French tragedy; but whether that is so or not, the point I want to make here is that if this element in Seneca's drama fitted in with sixteenth-century taste, then Seneca was a good model for sixteenth-century playwrights to choose. It seems clear that Seneca's *sententiæ* are in several respects in keeping with sixteenth-century taste. First, the Stoic message which emerges from them, or from a great number of them, namely that happiness is uncertain, Fortune capricious and unjust, suffering must be endured, courage is an almost divine virtue, would be acceptable in a period when the possibilities of neo-Stoicism were being explored.[1] It could even be adapted to religious plays, including those by Calvinists, since there is an easy *rapprochement* (though it is one which was repudiated by Calvin) between predestination and the Stoic idea of *Fatum*.[2] Although some of Seneca's *sententiæ*, for instance those on suicide, have to be suppressed or remodelled by French writers, many can be taken over without alteration into a Christian framework.

Secondly, the presence of these *sententiæ* in a play is likely to win the approval of the sixteenth-century educated public, whose theorists said that tragedy should be didactic. If it is studded with *sententiæ* a play can be didactic in two ways at once: the whole work can convey a message by showing the fall of a great prince or the wicked folly of questioning the ways of God, and meanwhile the *sententiæ* can cover a wider field of subjects and at the same time make more pointed and precise statements about them than the general assertion which is made by the whole theme and direction of a play.

Thirdly, the *sententiæ* are an important element in the rhetoric. It is as *beaux vers* as well as for their moral content that they are emphasized by typographical devices such as quotation marks or a contrasting type-face. They provide a mould which can easily be used to form new specimens, and some of the *sentences* in French plays which sound most proverbial, and which one might imagine to be translations, are in fact original. We can judge of the success which the *sententiæ* in Seneca and the *sentences* in French dramatists had with the reading public from the way in which anthologies were made of them, and collections of them were used as school-books because they exemplified both sound moral principles and fine style. Seneca was one of the main sources of *sententiæ*. The anthologist Mirandula, for example, quotes from a score of authors, but

---

[1] For an analysis of Seneca's *sententiæ*, see Paul Kahnt, *Der Gedankenkreis der Sentenzen in Jodelle's und Garnier's Tragödien und Seneca's Einfluss auf denselben* (Marburg, 1887).

[2] See L. Zanta, *La Renaissance du stoïcisme au XVIe siècle* (Paris, 1914).

well over a tenth of his quotations are from Seneca. Not all his quotations are *sententiæ*, of course—some are merely elegant ways of saying things, or neat definitions; but most of the Senecan quotations are sententious.[1]

In addition to a liking for the didactic, one is conscious when considering sixteenth-century taste of a certain largeness of scale—large emotions, heroism, even a certain flamboyance, are valued. This is borne out by the lavish pomp of state occasions or royal *entrées*, by the Pléiade's wish for a national epic, by Rabelais's giants and D'Aubigné's huge nightmare visions. Seneca provides a gallery of 'large' characters, high in rank and unique in achievement, capable of monstrous cruelty, supreme courage and extremes of all kinds—Hippolytus is ultra-chaste, Hercules is a demigod, literally superhuman, Medea is the extreme expression of the idea of the wronged woman, Hecuba experiences bereavements and grief of unique bitterness. Seneca's rhetoric is on an equally large scale; it is complicated, embodying countless elaborate figures and devices, and it is loud—there are few passages in Seneca that could satisfactorily be delivered other than in a shout. The sixteenth century takes over the largeness of the characters and the violence of the rhetoric.

This larger-than-life-size quality of the characters is partly responsible for one aspect of the kind of 'Senecan drama' seen in England, and also in French drama as late as Corneille. In Elizabethan drama, as in Corneille, we are aware of an element of display. 'Display' passages may seem similar to, but are not in fact serving the same purpose as, exposition scenes in the usual sense of that term. Thus the famous and much-imitated speech by Atreus in *Thyestes* which begins:

> Aequalis astris gradior et cunctos super
> altum superbo vertice attingens polum

is a display passage.[2] It is not exposition; the most striking lines in it tell us little about the situation in which Atreus finds himself. Nor is it an 'overheard' monologue, a device for letting us know

---

[1] Octavianus Mirandula, *Illustrium poëtarum flores* (Lyon, 1553).

[2] *Thyestes*, 885 *ff*. It is imitated by, e.g., Garnier in *Les Juifves*, Act II.

11

the secret thoughts of a character. It is Atreus telling us what he is like, speaking as we expect a tyrant to speak, labelling himself, giving a firm outline to his own figure. Seneca's characters all have this sharp-edged quality, there is nothing mysterious or ambiguous about them; the display speech is one method of achieving this clarity, and is a device which is taken over by imitators of Seneca. A seventeenth-century example can be seen in Corneille. The first speech made by Cléopâtre in *Rodogune* (Act I, scene i) is much more than a 'realistic' presentation of an ambitious, unscrupulous woman. After what we have already heard about Cléopâtre, we know that she is wicked and cruel; in this speech she displays herself to the audience, she speaks as we expect such a person to speak, and makes as it were a ritual renunciation of normal moral sanctions:

> Serments fallacieux, salutaire contrainte,
> Que m'imposa la force et qu'accepta ma crainte,
> Heureux déguisements d'un immortel courroux,
> Vains fantômes d'Etat, évanouissez-vous!
>
> (395–8)

She sums up in half a line her two preoccupations:

> Je hais, je règne encore.
>
> (411)

She becomes, more than an individual character, a larger-than-life figure, a type, a recognizable conventional creation talking as such a type is known to talk. Similarly when Nabuchodonosor begins a speech with:

> Pareil aux dieux je marche

or with:

> Je le tiens, je le tiens, je tiens la bête prise

this should not be treated as material from which to deduce what Nabuchodonosor is like as a person; that he is guilty of enormous *hubris*; that he takes a savage delight in the sufferings of his victims. On the contrary, the reaction of the audience should surely be one of recognition—we now see that Nabuchodonosor fits into a certain familiar category, that of the boastful, bullying tyrant; he speaks in the way proper to such a character.

This convention certainly stems from Seneca, although the matter may be very different; indeed it is generally true that the Senecan matter (Greek legend and Roman history) is less important in later Senecan drama, particularly in England, than Senecan form—dramatic conventions, rhetoric, pathos, *sententiæ*.

Another important characteristic of sixteenth-century drama is the retention of certain Senecan characters, more or less disguised. Amital loses none of her force when we realize that she is a Hecuba-figure, indeed the creation perhaps gains in stature when phrases such as

> Je suis le malheur même

recall Hecuba's claim to be the embodiment of extreme and utter grief; as in these lines in Seneca's *Troades*:

> Quoscumque luctus fleveris, flebis meos;
> sua quemque tantum, me omnium clades premit;
> mihi cuncta pereunt: quisquis est Hecubae est miser.
>
> (1060–2)

Amital becomes a more, not a less impressive character because of these resonances. The tyrant is another Senecan figure used repeatedly in sixteenth-century tragedy, although another element enters into the composition of some sixteenth-century tyrants: they are partly Machiavellian. It is a difficult task to disentangle the Machiavellian from the Senecan elements in the villains of sixteenth-century theatre, for the Senecan tyrant can be as cunning as a Machiavellian (Aegisthus, Atreus, Lycus) and may even invoke the *raison d'état*. The question has been examined for English tragedy, where the Machiavellians distinguish themselves by the use of such 'Italian' methods as killing by poison.[1] This criterion does not apply to French drama (the

---

[1] W. A. Armstrong, 'The Elizabethan conception of the tyrant', in *R.E.S.*, vol. XXII (1946), p. 161; by the same author, 'The influence of Seneca and Machiavelli on the Elizabethan tyrant,' in *R.E.S.*, vol. XXIV (1948), p. 19; also Mario Praz, 'The Politic brain: Machiavelli and the Elizabethans', reprinted in *The Flaming Heart* (New York, 1958) pp. 90–145.

use of poison in, for instance, Mellin de Saint Gelais's *Sophonisbe* could hardly be described as Machiavellian), but we may nevertheless find some Machiavellian elements in French drama; it would be surprising if this were not so, considering the popularity of Innocent Gentillet's *Contremachiavel* and the recurring accusation in polemical literature that Catherine de Médicis was a keen student of Machiavelli. But even with this possible addition of a tinge of 'Italian' subtlety or pragmatism, the basic material of the tyrant in sixteenth-century tragedy is Senecan, and the use of this and other stock characters represents another real debt of sixteenth-century tragedy to Seneca.

This outline of those elements of Senecan drama which proved fruitful sources of inspiration to sixteenth-century dramatists should suffice to indicate that the influence of Seneca on early classical tragedy was by no means so disastrous as has sometimes been suggested. In many respects his work suited contemporary tastes and in any case he was undoubtedly an easier model for writers to turn to than the Greeks would have been, with their greater difficulties both of language and thought.

HOW SENECAN IS 'SENECAN' DRAMA?

It now has to be seen how adequate it is to regard sixteenth-century French tragedy as 'Senecan'. It seems reasonable to take this point of view as a starting point, because of the presence in the plays of all the Senecan elements discussed above. It is certainly fairer and less anachronistic than judging the plays by seventeenth-century criteria. It is an approach which is genuinely relevant to the concerns and intentions of the sixteenth-century dramatists themselves, since they were consciously taking Seneca as their pattern. It will prepare us for some of the characteristics of sixteenth-century tragedy which may jar most when we approach it from a seventeenth-century or modern standpoint: the rhetorical use of language; the stress on an external Fate (or an inscrutable God who replaces the Fate of the ancients) as the controlling force shaping the action, rather than an action springing from internal forces of character; the doom-laden atmosphere and the use of supernatural elements such as ghosts, Furies or visions; the didactic nature of the drama; the lack of (or freedom from) any striving for 'convincing' or logical characters, since on the one hand the characters tend to be types, and on the other, their speeches are often set-pieces embodying a clearly defined and recognizable theme or mood, so that the nearest we come to delineation of character is the presentation of a series of moods.

Nevertheless, useful as it is, this Senecan approach can only be a starting point and will not provide a completely satisfactory way of looking at the plays.

One of its defects has been mentioned already: that it can result in the assumption that, for example, Garnier's *Hippolyte* is a translation of Seneca's *Hippolytus*, a view which is sometimes carried to the extreme of dismissing Garnier as a 'mere' Senecan dramatist.

Secondly, the Senecan approach seems to be partly responsible for the long controversy as to the 'stageability' of Garnier and other sixteenth-century playwrights. Seneca wrote closet drama —and this is presumably one reason why his theatre is so rhetorical and his descriptions of physical suffering so detailed and bloody. Passages such as that describing the murder of Agamemnon (*Agamemnon*, 901–5), or the still more revolting description of Atreus cooking his nephews (*Thyestes*, 759–67), exhibit a brutality and gruesomeness not to be equalled in sixteenth-century tragedy. Sometimes Seneca's use of the horrible is so exaggerated that it becomes ludicrous: one is grateful to Garnier for suppressing, in his *Hippolyte*, the grotesque passage in which Theseus, urged on by the chorus, tries to put together the fragments of Hippolytus's mangled body. Such excesses in Seneca are understandable: because he has no visible action, no visible characters to hold interest and rouse emotion, all his effects have to be achieved through a heightened and violent use of language. The sixteenth-century French dramatists, although they were imitating closet drama, seem clearly to have been thinking in terms of stage performance. Their own writings make this plain, and it is now accepted that many of these plays were in fact staged, in schools and colleges or elsewhere.[1]

Thirdly, the stress on Seneca as the main source for sixteenth-century tragedy may make us assume that the same ingredients were used in the same way by Seneca and by his French imitators. Thus the themes of Fate and Fortune, debates about kingship and the rights and duties of a king, and a great deal of physical cruelty, are all to be found in Seneca and in the French writers, and it is easy to assume, because they are expressed in similar terms, that they have the same purpose (or lack of purpose) in French as in Latin. This need not be so, and perhaps the greatest drawback of the Senecan approach is that it hinders an appreciation of the variations which French writers compose on their Senecan themes, and the different uses which they make of material borrowed from Seneca.

There are large and obvious differences between the situation and attitudes of Seneca and of his French admirers, and the two sets of plays are consequently different in emphasis, feeling and intention. The French dramatists often have either Protestant or royalist affiliations, they are writing for an audience which is well-read in the classics and respects the efforts of Jodelle, Garnier and other writers to renew the tradition of tragedy with French plays on the classical model; and several of them, but particularly Garnier, choose themes which reflect the situation in France—rebellion and civil war, with all the bitterness, cruelty and misery which these entail. Seneca is attached to the imperial household and unlikely to be able to deal with any pressing contemporary problems (the only play with direct reference to contemporary events, the *Octavia*, is almost certainly not by Seneca).[2] He is either catering to a taste for cruelty in imperial Rome, or is himself fascinated by suffering, for there is in his plays a repellent emphasis on physical cruelty and torture.

---

[1] See G. Lanson, *Esquisse d'une histoire de la tragédie française*, 2nd edition (Paris, 1954) pp. 27–32; Jules Haraszti, 'La littérature dramatique au temps de la Renaissance considérée dans ses rapports avec la scène contemporaine', *compte-rendu* in *R.H.L.F.*, vol. XI (1904), p. 680; various articles by R. Lebègue and E. Rigal (see bibliography).

[2] Elsewhere I treat the *Octavia* as part of the Senecan corpus, because it was regarded as authentic in the sixteenth century and therefore has to be considered in any discussion of Senecan influence.

He is a Stoic, with occasional moments, in the plays, of Epicurean feeling, whereas the French writers are Christian.

If we look in detail at some of the Senecan ingredients in French tragedy, we shall see how they are reworked to fit into this different framework of belief and attitude.

One of the most frequently recurring themes in Seneca is that of man's helplessness before the inscrutable and capricious forces of Fate and Chance. This indeed produces some of his finest lines, free from his two stylistic extremes of windy periphrasis and epigrammatic curtness:

> Fatis agimur; cedite fatis.
> non sollicitae possunt curae
> mutare rati stamina fusi.
> quidquid patimur mortale genus,
> quidquid facimus venit ex alto,
> servatque suae decreta colus
> Lachesis nulla revoluta manu.
>
>   (*Oedipus*, 980–6, Chorus)

>   novit paucos
> secura quies, qui velocis
> memores aevi, tempora numquam
> reditura tenent. dum fata sinunt,
> vivite laeti. properat cursu
> vita citato, volucrique die
> rota praecipitis vertitur anni.
> durae peragunt pensa sorores,
> nec sua retro fila revolvunt.
> at gens hominum fertur rapidis
> obvia fatis, incerta sui:
> Stygias ultro quaerimus undas.
>
>   (*Hercules furens*, 175–86, Chorus)

French writers usually transmit only as much of such philosophical themes in Seneca as can be absorbed into a Christian neo-Stoic framework. In Garnier's religious tragedy, Fate becomes identified with the often inscrutable will of God, as in lines 373–4 of *Les Juifves*:

17

helas! ciel endurci
Quand seras-tu lassé de me gesner ici?

The same thing happens in La Taille's *Saül le furieux* where
Saül states that man cannot resist the will of God, in terms that
echo those used by Seneca in speaking about Fate:

Je sçay bien qu'aux mortels appeller il ne faut
De son Arrest fatal decidé de la haut.
(*Saül le furieux*, 399–400)

And later in this same play the chorus of Levites offers another
version of the 'fatis agimur; cedite fatis' of Seneca in Christian
(and specifically Calvinist) terms:

S'il est ainsi ne murmurons
Mais patiemment endurons
Tout cela qui vient de sa main,
Soit rigoureux ou soit humain.
(*Ibid.*, 897–900)

The *topos* of Fortune and her wheel sometimes appears un-
transformed, in straight 'pagan' terms, even in a biblical play.
Thus the Escuyer in *Saül le furieux*:

Ha Sort leger, flateur, traistre et muable,
Tu monstres bien que ta Roue est variable.
(*Ibid.*, 1305–6)

But in Garnier, Fortune is replaced by God, or the theme is
linked to a cyclical theory of history and to the morally edifying
theme of the fall of a mighty man; thus in a speech made to
Nabuchodonosor by his Queen, God replaces Fortune and the
spectacle of Sédécie's fall is pointed out as a warning:

Dieu rabaisse le coeur des Monarques hautains
Qui s'egalent à luy, et qui n'ont cognoissance
Que tout humain pouvoir provient de sa puissance.
Vous voyez par ce Roy (dont les ancestres ont
Porté si longuement le diadème au front,
Et ores vostre esclave, accablé de miseres)
Combien les Royautez sont choses passageres.
(*Les Juifves*, Act iii, 930–6)

Again, the sixteenth-century dramatists, following Seneca,

18

choose kings and rulers as their principal characters. Here we notice a possibility of Senecan drama which is exploited neither by Seneca nor by most of his imitators in sixteenth-century France. In Seneca, the fact that the characters are princes merely makes them more imposing, gives them greater power to hurt and a greater height from which to fall. Their political commitments are of much less importance than their private revenges. Thus Atreus, the villain-hero of Seneca's *Thyestes*, is, like Garnier's Nabuchodonosor, a ferocious, bloodthirsty king; but his quarrel with Thyestes is a personal quarrel and his actions are dictated by a desire for personal revenge on his brother, who has done him a personal wrong. This is true of most of Seneca's monstrous bullies and tyrants, and the influence of this aspect of Senecan drama is seen in the Elizabethan revenge tragedy. Nabuchodonosor, on the contrary, is not avenging a personal wrong so much as punishing a political crime and dealing with a rebellious subject. He lets personal animosity and blood-thirstiness influence his actions, but the origin of his quarrel with Sédécie is political. As an example of the way in which other sixteenth-century writers failed to exploit the possibilities of their use of 'grands seigneurs' (the expression used by Jean de la Taille in *L'Art de la Tragédie*), we might consider Montchrestien's *L'Escossaise*: in the first act of this play there is a discussion between Elizabeth and a Counsellor about whether it is morally right and politically expedient to execute Marie Stuart, and one has the impression that this might be a play about the *raison d'état*, or about the particular kind of moral decisions which sovereigns have to make. But Montchrestien, following the line provided by his source (Pierre Matthieu's *Histoire des derniers troubles de France*) abandons this theme.[1] Elizabeth disappears from the play and we are concerned only with Marie Stuart's *constance* in the face of death, leading to rhetorical developments of great beauty on subjects such as the brevity of life:

Quand une fois la mort flestrit nostre paupiere,

[1] Montchrestien's use of Pierre Matthieu is pointed out by Frances A. Yates, 'Some new light on *L'Ecossaise* of Antoine de Montchrestien', in *M.L.R.*, vol. xxii (1927) p. 285.

Yeux, vous pouvez bien dire: adieu, douce clarté.
La vie est sans arrest, et si court à son terme
D'un mouvement si prompt qu'on ne l'apperçoit point;
Là si tost qu'elle arrive elle y demeure ferme,
Le naistre et le mourir est presque un mesme poinct.

Thus Montchrestien, like Seneca, seems to use the rank of his characters only to lend them greater dignity, and the same might be said of most other sixteenth-century dramatists. But Buchanan, La Taille and Garnier are all interested in the political commitments of their characters. In George Buchanan's New Testament tragedy *Baptistes*, we find Herod expressing the thoughts of a good king.[1] He describes the agonizing form that patriotism takes for a king—identification with his people to the point where the loss of a subject is felt as a personal wound:

> infima quoties perit
> De plebe quisquam, corporis membrum mei
> Toties revelli existimo: meus cruor
> Mitti videtur.

He defines the difference between a good king and a tyrant:

> Nempe hoc tyrannos interest regi bono,
> Hic servat hostes, hostis ille civium est.

These, and other passages where he discusses kingship and argues with his queen, are not purely rhetorical developments of stock Senecan themes, but are strictly relevant to the plot and have, in addition, an ironical force in that Herod is a tyrant who finds it expedient, in his political manoeuvring, to pose as a good king. This provides an effect of dramatic contrast when the king finally reveals himself as a tyrant, rejecting normal moral sanctions and declaring of such moral ties as friendship or loyalty to family:

> pauperum
> Sunt vincla: vana regibus vocabula.
> Nil arbitretur turpe, quod regi utile.

[1] George Buchanan, *Baptistes, sive Calumnia* (London, 1577) pp. 22, 25. Although Buchanan was a Scot, and wrote his plays in Latin, it seems relevant to include him in this study, because he lived and taught in France and his plays were performed there.

In La Taille's *Saül le furieux*, also, Saül's kingship is important not just as a rhetorical theme, or as a means of heightening the dignity of the personage, but as a central element in the play; one of the dominant themes, and springs of the action, is Saül's concern that he has led his people into a disastrous plight and, though responsible for them, feels himself helpless to rescue them. Linked with this is his resentment at having had kingship thrust upon him by God, and then having been allowed, or forced, by God to fail as a king:

> O grandeur malheureuse, en quel gouffre de mal
> M'abismes-tu helas, ô faulx degré Royal!
> Mais qu'avois-je offensé quand de mon toict champestre
> Tu me tiras, ô Dieu, envieux de mon estre,
> Où je vivois content sans malediction . . .
>
> Tu me fis sacrer Roy, tu me haulsas espres
> A fin de m'enfondrer en mil malheurs apres!
> Veux-tu donc (inconstant) piteusement destruire
> Le premier Roy qu'au monde il pleut à toy d'eslire!
> (*Saül le furieux*, 793–7, 809–12)

Thus these writers, while taking over from Seneca the convention of writing tragedy only about princes and great men, have exploited some possibilities of this convention that Seneca ignores.

Another feature of Senecan drama which sixteenth-century dramatists take over is closely connected to the last: it is the incorporation into the tragedy of many passages about political problems and in particular about the nature and duties of kingship. Such passages occur in Seneca even though he does not develop the dramatic possibilities inherent in the high political rank of his protagonists, and they include several which, taken together, give a picture of the ideal king; among these passages are Andromache's pathetic evocation of the kingly offices which Astyanax will never be able to perform (*Troades*, 771–4), Seneca's list of the royal qualities in which his pupil Nero is conspicuously deficient (*Octavia*, 472–91), Jocasta's exhortation to Oedipus to behave with the courage and steadfast attitude to Fortune which are becoming in a king (*Oedipus*, 81–5), Atreus's assumption of regal generosity (*Thyestes*, 529, 534), Medea's attempt to make Creon practise the royal virtues of slowness to anger, benevolence and protection of the weak (*Medea*, 203–25) and Theseus's description of what happens to good kings after death (*Hercules furens*, 739–47). Nowhere in Seneca does a good king appear in person. Tyrants, on the contrary, abound; Atreus, Nero, Lycus, Aegisthus all embody this type, whose character-istics are shown to be extreme cruelty (*Agamemnon*, 994–6; *Hercules furens*, 511–13; *Thyestes*, 246–8, 1065–8), stark un-reasonableness and injustice (*Octavia*, 863–7), the firm belief that a king must take revenge on his enemies (*Thyestes*, 176–8) and the destructive will, envious of anything which could pos-sibly offer a threat to the tyrant's power (*Octavia*, 492–8). Seneca also deals with the question of why a king becomes a tyrant (power and success corrupt—*Agamemnon*, 247–52), with the double theme of the lure and the dangers or burdens of king-ship (in every play except *Hippolytus*) and with the circular argument about the relationship of king to populace—whether to rule by fear or love, with force or kindness; for an exposition of the whole insoluble problem, see *Octavia*, especially the pass-age of stichomythia between Nero and Seneca in the first episode, 440–61.[1]

But although there are so many *sententiæ* and other passages about kingship and certain other political topics (notably war and the wickedness of courts), it should not be assumed that such passages are as important in Seneca as they are in Garnier. For one thing, although these passages seem abundant when catalogued as in the last paragraph, they are not numerically more important than those on Fortune, the nature of the human condition, or the delights of *aurea mediocritas*. Also, they are not necessary to the plays in which they occur (with the exception, perhaps, of the Nero-Seneca debate in *Octavia*). They are rele-vant only in so far as the presentation of, for example, Atreus's extreme delight in cruelty adds to the horror inspired by the whole subject of *Thyestes*. When a political subject is debated, the out-come of the debate will not normally have any effect on the plot, so that the argument appears to have none but a rhetorical value.

[1] Quoted in chapter 6, p. 105.

Alternatively, a political topic may be looked at or developed in such a way that it ceases to be purely political and becomes of general human or philosophical interest. This happens in Jocasta's exhortation to Oedipus when her statement that a king should have a courageous attitude to Fortune is followed by the line:

> Haud est virile terga Fortunae dare
>
> (*Oedipus*, 86)

which links this standard to a more general code. The same thing occurs in a choral definition of kingship:

> mens regnum bona possidet . . .
> rex est qui metuit nihil,
> rex est qui cupiet nihil.
> hoc regnum sibi quisque dat.
>
> (*Thyestes*, 380, 388–90)

One has here the impression that Seneca is using the king as an image of the Stoic sage, just as elsewhere he uses an image from the other end of the political hierarchy, the figure of the honest, unambitious countryman, as the embodiment of true wisdom, suggesting by this double image, the king and the peasant, that the sage is independent of external conditions, that the Stoic ideal is designed for the inner life, which is within human control while the blows of Fortune are not.[1]

In fact, Seneca's aim and emphasis are not political. The degree to which political themes are integrated into the drama varies greatly; one or two are fairly central: Nero's tyranny is essential to the *Octavia* and the debates between him and his tutor Seneca, and between him and his captain, are relevant and unforced. Sometimes a political theme is introduced for dramatic or ironic effect: Atreus's deceptively generous words about kingship in *Thyestes*, and the passage in *Medea* where Medea, who for love has completely abandoned the moral code, argues

---

[1] Cf. also *Thyestes*, 342–68, where the distinguishing characteristic of a king is declared to be not wealth, nor the wearing of imperial purple and a diadem, nor a sumptuous style of living, but the mind which is free from fear and ambition, is unmoved by popular fickleness, by avarice, or by threats of force and willingly accepts its fate; as in the other passages quoted, this moves from political considerations to general moralizing, applicable to all men and not exclusively to kings.

with Creon the case for a noble, highly moral conception of kingship. But most political passages have little dramatic justification; they have no unique relevance to the situation in which they occur, but would be equally appropriate at another point or in another play.[1]

Were all the political elements in Seneca's plays integrated into the structure and movement of the drama, one might conclude that an awareness of political problems and conflicts lay at the heart of Seneca's tragic vision. Were they all extraneous, one might perhaps suppose him to be trying to awaken interest in political problems, and sugaring the pill by inserting his political views in tragedies.

The only reasonable interpretation must, I think, lie aside from either of these hypothetical extremes.

Seneca's tragedies are first and foremost linguistic and rhetorical exercises; his main preoccupation is with problems of style and expression. In so far as there is any 'message' or thought-content in these plays, it is not political, but lies in the presentation of a pessimistic view of the human condition. Political themes are used occasionally because they are appropriate to the drama, more often because they fit in with Seneca's gloomy view of life (ambition, the lure and burden of kingship, the corrupting influence of power, the vulnerability of the great, the need for a king to be either fearful or feared), or can be linked to his answer to the admitted atrociousness of life (Stoic fortitude and self-sufficiency, Epicurean retreat into poverty or obscurity), or provide a suitable theme for a rhetorical flourish (the Golden Age, the joys of political obscurity, described by an uninvolved chorus). The 'moelle substantifique' of the plays lies in those moments of peaceful reflection (which F. L. Lucas has described as falling 'like a blessed quiet across the shriekings and stridencies of Seneca's usual *fortissimo*') when Seneca allows us to remember that he is primarily a philosopher.[2]

In short, although Seneca's plays contain a certain amount of

---

[1] E.g., many chorus meditations on changing fortunes in war, or the happiness of life free from political entanglements; or Seneca's disquisition, in *Octavia*, on the Golden Age, with a summary of the subsequent history of the world (*Octavia*, 400–35).

[2] F. L. Lucas, *Seneca and Elizabethan tragedy* (Cambridge, 1922), p. 72.

political material, he is not a political dramatist. This does not mean that all French writers who follow Seneca in embodying political material in their plays do so for the same, mainly rhetorical, purpose; in criticism of sixteenth-century drama it is a danger of the Senecan approach that it encourages such an assumption.

So although Seneca's influence was in many respects a positive gain to the early development of French tragedy, and although it is important to realize the extent of this influence and the degree to which sixteenth-century French tragedy is conventional and rhetorical, it is equally important not to stop short at this realization, but to take into account the ways in which sixteenth-century writers, even while using 'Senecan' elements in their plays, can produce quite un-Senecan results.

3

POLITICAL AIMS AND ALLUSIONS

If the Senecan approach to Garnier is not entirely satisfactory, what reasons are there for supposing that a political one would be more fruitful? Has Garnier a political message? The evidence suggesting that he has is of various kinds. In this chapter I propose first to look at what one might call the 'external' evidence of Garnier's political tendencies, then to examine to what degree, if any, one can connect the plays with specific contemporary events, and lastly to discuss whether the known facts of Garnier's life permit any surmise as to his political views, and if so, whether they confirm what emerges from the rest of the investigation.

The first important piece of 'external' evidence is the fact that other people of his own time thought of Garnier as a political writer. In the rare Saumur edition of Garnier's plays (Arsenal Rf 1249) are an 'avis sur les tragédies de R. Garnier' and an ode whose author has been identified by V.-L. Saulnier as Etienne Gasteuil.[1] This writer praises Garnier not for literary excellence but for reminding the French people of other periods of civil wars and of 'le meutre et infidelité' and thus providing a useful political lesson. There are suggestions of the same theme in other *liminaires* to Garnier's plays, particularly in those by Pierre Amy. In some lines on *Cornélie* he writes:

> Vivunt reclusis, vindice te, fatis patres
>   Pro patria audaces mori,
> Vivunt, tuoque numine, opima spiritus
>   Atrocis exempla invidae
> Oblivioni detrahunt: quae vel truces
>   Posthac tyrannos terreant.

(Pinvert, p. 91)

[1] V.–L. Saulnier, 'Un Ami inconnu de Robert Garnier, le poète Etienne Gasteuil', in *Revue Universitaire*, vol. LXI (1952), p. 88, and 'Etienne Gasteuil, apologiste de Robert Garnier', in *Bulletin du bibliophile et du bibliothécaire*, no. 3 (1959), p. 105.

The idea expressed in 'quae . . . posthac tyrannos terreant' is found again in Amy's anagram of Garnier's name: 'Vanis terror regibus' (Pinvert, p. 167). Jacques Liger, in his *liminaire* to *Cornélie*, mentions the civil war theme before, and as though it is more important than, Cornélie's grief:

> Civilis rabiem furoris acri
> Inflatus numeris quatis Camoena,
> Et Corneliam inauspicata flentem
> Pompei arma, fugam necemque patris.
>
> (Pinvert, pp. 91–2)

Thus Garnier's preoccupation with political subjects, and the possible didactic value of his plays as political propaganda, seem to have struck his contemporaries.

A second kind of evidence is that of Garnier's own prefaces. Here it is illuminating to compare what Garnier says about his plays with what other writers have said when discussing or describing tragedies in general. We have already seen that Ronsard calls the two dramatic forms 'didascaliques et enseignantes'. Jean Antoine de Baïf is somewhat more precise as to the possible nature of the 'enseignement'; in his *Epistre au Roy*, a work which amounts to an *institution du prince*, he recommends the young king (Henri III) to watch tragedies because they deal with the lives of kings and will therefore be instructive for him.[1] But this is still vague, and suggestive of a philosophical or moral lesson rather than political instruction. When we come, however, to the preface of *Cornélie*, we find that Garnier says he is writing tragedies because they are the *genre* most suited to the times in which he lives ('poème à mon regret trop propre aux malheurs de nostre siècle').[2] This explanation is repeated in the dedications of *La Troade* and *Les Juifves* and implied in that to *Marc-Antoine*. There is also an interesting text in the form of a *liminaire* which Garnier wrote for the *Hymnes de Synese* translated by Jacques de Courtin de Cissé, in which he gives this account of his own literary activity:

> Tandis qu'en durs regrets, et en plaintes ameres

[1] J. A. de Baïf, *Epistre au Roy, sous le nom de la Royne sa mere* (Paris, 1575).
[2] Pinvert, p. 90.

Tu me vois lamenter d'une tragique voix
Les desastres Romains, et les mal-heurs Gregeois,
Pleurant nos propres maux sous feintes etrangeres . . .[1]

Garnier himself, then, seems to have felt that there was a close relationship between the events that form the setting of his plays, and those of the French wars of religion.

This leads us to the third piece of evidence: Garnier's choice of subjects. There must be more than coincidence in the fact that of Garnier's seven tragedies, three deal with various episodes of the Roman civil wars, one with the war of the Seven against Thebes (which was also a civil war, since a Theban prince was attacking Thebes), and two others (*La Troade* and *Les Juifves*) with the aftermath of war or rebellion.

From Garnier's remarks it seems legitimate to assume a connection between his choice of subjects and contemporary events. But the idea of such a connection must be handled cautiously as it can easily lead to unlikely conclusions.

Garnier's first play was published in 1568, his last in 1583; thus the period of his literary activity falls entirely within the confused and troubled decades of the wars of religion (1562–93). Detailed correlation between external events and parts of Garnier's plays is a risky undertaking because of the difficulty of dating the composition of the plays. M.-M. Mouflard has suggested dates, some of them considerably earlier than the date of publication; but her reasoning does not always seem convincing, so that one is bound to feel dubious about accepting her hypotheses.[2] Thus one might agree with her that *Marc-Antoine* was probably published early rather than late in 1578, on the evidence of the dedication, where Pibrac's promotion to *président du Parlement*, which had taken place in September 1577, is referred to as a recent honour. But I feel less happy about the suggestion that Amy's poem accompanying *Marc-Antoine*, and therefore

---

[1] See *Hymnes de Synese . . . traduits de grec en françois par Jaques de Courtin de Cissé, gentilhomme percheron* (Paris, 1581). Garnier's poem is also reprinted in Lebègue II, p. 243.

[2] Marie-Madeleine Mouflard, *Robert Garnier 1545–1590*, 3 vols. (La Ferté Bernard and La Roche sur Yon, 1961–64).

the play itself, was composed before the publication of Jodelle's *Cléopâtre* in 1574. The text of the ode does not seem to me to require this interpretation; the phrase 'non alio prius dictum ore' (Pinvert, p. 166) need not be taken as an exact and literal statement, but as a compliment to Garnier's supremacy. In any case, strictly speaking, Garnier *was* the first to write a play about Mark Antony—who is already dead at the beginning of Jodelle's play. Amy's phrase seems insufficient evidence for placing the composition of the play in the year 1574–5, especially as such a deduction implies that Amy did not know of Jodelle's play before it was published. Considering the stir caused by *Cléopâtre captive* at the time of its first performance in 1552, this seems unlikely. We are on equally uncertain ground with the attempt to date the play by tracing political allusions. On the basis of these it is suggested that 'Cléopâtre serait la belle Marie Stuart et Antoine soit Darnley, soit Bothwell, soit les deux', but there is little in the play to support this uneasy claim.[1] The choice of subject does not seem to need such strained explanation in view of the existence of Jodelle's play and Plutarch's account of the last days of Antony and Cleopatra. Moreover, Garnier deals here with the final phase of the Roman civil wars, of which he had treated two earlier moments in *Porcie* and *Cornélie*, so that this play is a logical third member of the group.

I find it similarly hard to believe, with M.-M. Mouflard, that *Les Juifves* presents the struggle between Henri, duc de Guise (Nabuchodonosor) and Henri III (Sédécie), who has disregarded the advice of Catherine de Médicis (Amital).[2] Nabuchodonosor is Sédécie's overlord, holding absolute and undisputed power over him; this in my opinion is an important aspect of the political situation in *Les Juifves*, but one that has to be ignored if the play is to be given this specific, and restrictive, interpretation. Moreover, the play was published before the 'guerre des trois Henri' when this conflict (between Guise and Henri III) became acute, and even before the Treaty of Joinville (December, 1584) by which the Catholic princes formed themselves into the 'Sainte Ligue' and their hostility to Henri III became manifest. The play was probably written at a time when

[1] *Ibid.*, *Robert Garnier. La Vie*, p. 337.   [2] *Ibid.*, p. 343.

Henri III's ambitious and unreliable younger brother, François, duc d'Anjou (formerly duc d'Alençon) was a much more pressing problem than Guise. Nor did Henri take any bold political action seriously opposed to his mother's advice until the murder of the Duc de Guise in 1588.

On the other hand, if this *pièce à clé* interpretation of the plays is unsatisfactory, some approximate correlations may still be suggested. If we look at the plays in their chronological order we shall see what possible connections they have with contemporary events.

Porcie may have been written during the second civil war, but more probably during the uneasy years between the first and second wars (1563–7). This precarious peace was interrupted by violent incidents, as in June 1566 at Pamiers (Pyrenees), when Catholics molested Protestants, and in retaliation the Protestants attacked monasteries in the district; the situation finally exploded with the 'Entreprise de Meaux' (September, 1567), when the Protestants tried to seize the young king, as Guise had done previously at Fontainebleau; during the general Protestant revolt which followed this there occurred the gruesome 'Michelade de Nîmes' when eighty notable Catholics, monks and priests were massacred. Thus even while technically no war was in progress, the threat of war was never far away, and the memory of the last war was kept alive by the constant local outbreaks of violence. In connection with this, the first thing to notice about *Porcie* is the use Garnier makes of its civil war setting. Such a setting is common to several of the plays, and is of contemporary relevance every time it appears. But it is worth remarking, in this first use of it, how fully Garnier exploits the theme, bringing everything back to this point of reference. One example of this can be seen in the treatment of the *aurea mediocritas* commonplace, imitated from Horace, *Epodes* II; when this occurs in *Porcie* (Act II, p. 27), the envied escape is not from corruption in cities or at court, nor from the weary burden of public office, nor from the blows of fortune to which high rank exposes a man, but from 'la civile fureur', 'la trompette armant l'assaut', 'le danger de l'alarme'. Similarly, the lament after Porcie's death is very largely a lament over Rome and the pitiable condition to which the civil war has reduced it:

NOURRICE: Plorez vostre cité, mes fidèles compagnes.

(Act v, p. 82)

If the theme of civil war controls to a large extent the rhetorical colouring of the play, the other central theme, that of tyrannicide, dominates its intellectual and argumentative side. But here I think there is only a negative point to make about this: after the massacre of St Bartholomew (August, 1572) this theme became a real political (and theological) issue and many Protestant works discussed the question of tyrannicide and justified it, morally and legally. After that date, and before the reversal of opinion prompted by the death of François, duc d'Anjou in 1584 (which left a Protestant as heir presumptive to the throne), it would have been surprising to find anyone without strong Protestant sympathies contemplating tyrannicide as calmly as Garnier appears to do in this play. He is able to do this only because the subject has not yet become a dangerous one in France. It is true that Porcie finally declares that it was a mistake to kill Caesar—but not because it was wrong, only because it was pointless; and there is a strong current of admiration for the conspirators, and of sympathy with their noble and public-spirited intentions. They meant well, says Porcie, but their heroism was a senseless waste, because Rome is worse off now than under Caesar.

Garnier's second play, *Hippolyte*, is not a political play. M.-M. Mouflard has a theory that he altered it, after the Saint-Barthélemy and before publication, to cut out passages which might seem to refer to the massacre.[1] This theory is unproved and, in the absence of manuscript evidence, unprovable. The nearest the play comes to political relevance is perhaps the social criticism in the nurse's speech to Phèdre, describing in censorious terms how the rich tend to seek out delicate, curious and forbidden pleasures because:

L'amour accoustumé luy desplaist trop vulgaire

[1] M.-M. Mouflard, *Robert Garnier. La Vie*, p. 333.

31

and because:

> Il veut s'ébatre d'un qui ne soit ordinaire,
> Qui ne soit naturel, mais tout incestueux,
> Mais tout abominable, horrible et monstrueux.
> Tousjours, tousjours les grands ont leurs âmes esprises,
> Ont leur coeur enflammé de choses non permises.
> Celuy qui peut beaucoup veut encor plus pouvoir.
>
> (Act II, pp. 272–3)

The last line quoted suggests a ruler, rather than just any rich man, as it is reminiscent of other phrases used by or of kings in Garnier:

> *Aux Rois qui peuvent tout, toute chose est licite.*
> (Nabuchodonosor in *Les Juifves*, Act III, 924)
> *D'autant qu'il peut beaucoup, d'autant luy doit moins plaire.*
> (Agamemnon in *La Troade*, Act III, 1486)

In view of this, one wonders whether any conscious reference was intended here to Marguerite de Valois, and to the incest which she almost admits in her memoirs. Two years before her marriage to Henri de Navarre (the Scarlet Wedding which preceded the St Bartholomew massacre), she had been reprimanded by her brother and her mother for encouraging the attentions of the young Duc de Guise, but before that, it was rumoured that she and her brother (the future Henri III) were lovers.

The publication of *Cornélie* coincided approximately with the outbreak of the fifth civil war (*conspiration du mardi gras*, February, 1574), in which the royal forces were opposed by the *politiques*, the coalition of Protestants and malcontent Catholics, led by the Duc d'Alençon. Again therefore (as with *Porcie*), the writing was probably done during a period of uneasy peace, or else during the fourth war.

The numerous horrible descriptions of bloodshed in *Cornélie* may well reflect the particularly bloody incidents which followed the St Bartholomew massacre. (After 24 August, Charles IX sent contradictory and ambiguous orders, letters and messages to his provincial governors, and by many these were interpreted as instructions, or at any rate permission, to repeat the massacre in their own towns.)[1]

Cornélie contains several passages describing battle scenes, and even though three (p. 102, p. 134, p. 158) use the conventional battlefield-cornfield image (already briefly used in *Porcie*, p. 45, p. 50), the others are more descriptive and more horrible than anything in the earlier play; we are spared no detail of bloodshed, mutilation, and the groans of the dying. War, as Garnier shows us it in these descriptions, is not only dangerous, frightening and noisy; it is ugly and disgusting:

> On ne voyoit qu'horreur, que soldars encombrez
> Sous le faix des chevaux, que des corps démembrez
> Nageans dans leur sang propre, et des piles dressées
> D'hommes qui gémissoyent, sous les armes pressées,
> Coulant comme un esponge, ou l'amas raisineux
> Qu'un pesant fust escache en un pressouer vineux.
>
> (Act v, p. 159)

Garnier says in the dedication of *Cornélie* that this tragic poem is 'propre aux malheurs de nostre siècle', dealing as it does with a 'grande République rompue par l'ambicieux discord de ses citoyens', and in the play he shows the *continuity* of this discord: the struggle of Caesar against Pompey will be followed by that of Caesar against Brutus and Cassius. Three generations are represented in the play: Scipio, Caesar and Brutus. In the French civil wars, successive phases constantly revealed new partnerships and new enmities, and one generation handed on the quarrel to the next. When *Cornélie* appeared, the Duc de Guise, the King of Navarre and the Prince de Condé each represented the second generation of their families to play a prominent part in the struggle.

The references in *Cornélie* to tyrants and tyrannicide might appear bold, or might seem to place Garnier firmly in the Protestant camp, coming so soon after the St Bartholomew massacre. But 'tyrant' is used here in the sense of 'usurper';

[1] For details see S. L. England, *The Massacre of St Bartholomew*, (London, 1938) and Henri Noguères, *La Saint Barthélemy* (Paris, 1959).

Caesar is hated not for being a bad monarch, but for being a monarch at all—for illegitimately making himself a king in all but name. Thus, Garnier does not handle the explosive theme of the legitimate king who becomes a tyrant, which is the way Protestants saw Charles IX after the St Bartholomew massacre.

In May, 1574, Charles IX died and Garnier contributed two sonnets to his *Tombeau*, along with Ronsard and Jamyn.[1] In doing this, he was contributing to a piece of royal propaganda and allying himself with the defenders of Charles IX, whose name certainly needed defending. Wherever the real responsibility for the St Bartholomew massacre lay, Charles as sovereign was nominally responsible; 'Il a prêté son nom à un gouvernement qui n'était pas le sien, et sa timide velléité de pouvoir personnel n'a servi qu'à le déshonorer'.[2] One of Garnier's sonnets from the *Tombeau* also appeared, along with yet a third sonnet (Lebègue II, p. 240), in an account of Charles IX's death prepared by Arnaud Sorbin, Charles IX's chaplain.[3] This had a double propaganda aim: it was to scotch the rumours that Charles IX's last hours were haunted by guilty nightmare visions of the massacre of 1572; and it was to counteract the suspicion that the King's death had not been natural, but had been brought about by his mother.

Apart from these poems (probably commissioned) we know of nothing else written by Garnier before *Marc-Antoine* (published in 1578). The throne had been occupied for nearly four years by the much-maligned Henri III, a man of many qualities, by far the most intelligent of the Valois kings, courageous, imaginative, a born orator; but also neurotic, vain, probably a sexual pervert, and so vilified by his enemies that even now he tends to be seen in the distorting glass of their slander campaign as effeminate, cruel, vindictive and hypocritical—'the shadow of the Valois, yawning at the Mass' (G. K. Chesterton in 'Lepanto'). As Duc d'Anjou, he

[1] *Le Tombeau du feu Roy Tres Chrestien Charles IX* (Paris, 1574).

[2] Jean H. Mariéjol, *La Réforme et la Ligue* (vol. VI, part I of *Histoire de France depuis les origines jusqu'à la révolution*, ed. Ernest Lavisse (Paris, 1904) p. 152.

[3] *Le Vray discours des derniers propos memorables, et trespas du feu Roy de tres bonne memoire Charles neufiesme* (Paris, 1574).

was the hero of the battles of Jarnac (March ,1569) and Moncontour (October, 1569), but now, say his opponents, his extravagant
and voluptuous way of life has lost him the sympathy of his subjects. The parallel between Marc-Antoine and Henri III was
likely to occur to his readers, even if Garnier did not intend it;
but he probably did, for he would have had to be very unobser-
vant not to notice the obvious analogy. The criticism is in a
sense sympathetic—stress is laid on Marc-Antoine's past heroism
and glorious ancestry, and he is shown to be aware of his own
degeneration. Taken as criticism, it is within the limits of what
a crown officer might permit himself (Garnier was made *lieutenant criminel du Maine* in May, 1574), even an officer who has
already contributed to a piece of royal propaganda; a man indebted and openly committed to the house of Valois, but not, it
seems, uncritically so.

Henri III had had a serious rebuff at the Estates General held
at Blois (November, 1576–January, 1577); after taking great
pains to persuade the deputies to demand religious unity, which
inevitably meant war, he then could not induce them to vote
him enough money to carry on the war. This was the occasion
when, weeping with anger, he exclaimed as he left the session
'Ils ne veulent m'aider du leur ni permettre que je me secoure du
mien [by raising money on the royal domain]; c'est une trop
grande cruauté.' After this personal failure, and amid the flood
of vituperative pamphlet literature abusing Catherine, Henri,
the Italians and the *mignons*, we can perhaps see Garnier's
censure of the ruler who is weakened by *volupté* as a piece of
well-meant criticism and implied advice. Misgovernment, loss of
the sceptre to a 'main estrangère' (there was much resentment,
not limited to Protestants, at the power enjoyed by Guise, a
prince of Lorraine, and at the control of finance by the Italians),
leaving the people to the mercy of 'flateurs qui leur sucent les os',
injustice, disorder and finally rebellion: 'Voylà de Volupté les
effets dommageables' according to Garnier's Lucile (*Marc-
Antoine*, Act III, p. 210).

Apart from this allusion, the whole setting of the play
(another moment in the Roman civil wars) is of course still
relevant. This is worth pointing out because Garnier himself

emphasizes it in two ways. In his dedication to Guy du Faur de Pibrac (now back from Poland where he had been negotiating with the Poles to keep Henri III as their king, and newly appointed a *président du Parlement*), he writes: 'à qui mieux qu'à vous se doivent addresser les représentations tragiques des guerres civiles de Rome?' This indicates, firstly, that although the most obvious themes of the play are the Cléopâtre—Marc-Antoine relationship, and the fate of Egypt at the hands of the victorious Octavian, to Garnier this play belongs with the other civil war tragedies (*Porcie* and *Cornélie*); it concludes the series by showing the aftermath of the last incident in the civil wars, the battle of Actium. Secondly, Pibrac is a suitable person to whom to address such a play because, says Garnier, he is concerned about the 'dissentions domestiques et malheureux troubles' of modern France—which clearly shows that Garnier intends the reader to be aware of parallels between republican Rome and sixteenth-century France.

In addition to the criticism of a pleasure-loving ruler, another way in which *Marc-Antoine* links up with the French situation is in its references to foreign war. The theme that foreign war is preferable to civil war might have been relevant throughout the period, but particularly in 1571–2, when Admiral Coligny was planning an expedition to liberate the Low Countries, supporting his scheme with various arguments, one of which (and probably his main motive) was that foreign war united a country and put an end to civil dispute—a Machiavellian principle; and it was relevant again from 1576 onwards, when François, duc d'Anjou, adopted Coligny's views for his own ends. Coligny sought to end civil war in France; as a convinced Protestant, he would no doubt also have been happy to free the Dutch Protestants from the heavy rule of Catholic Spain. The Duc d'Anjou was, in theory at least, a Catholic; his main interest in a campaign in the Low Countries was that he hoped to find a throne for himself there; such a campaign might also improve his chances with the Protestant Elizabeth of England, François having succeeded Henri III as a candidate for her hand. His first expedition to the Low Countries was in July, 1578–January, 1579, and for some time before this he had been advocating the idea, certainly since

1576 when, after the death of Don Luis de Requesens in May, and the sack of Maestricht and Antwerp by mutinous Spanish troops, the Belgian Catholics had asked Anjou to protect them. In the summer of 1577, Marguerite de Valois, his sister (and Queen of Navarre) had travelled in the Low Countries on Anjou's behalf, to investigate what chances he had of acquiring sovereign power there. Henri III was not enthusiastic about his brother's activities in the Low Countries and was not convinced by Anjou's argument that it was a way of getting rid of hotheads who in Flanders could 'passer leur fumée et se saouler de la guerre.'[1] Garnier had already used an expression similar to this, on the same subject, in his first play, *Porcie*:

> C'est aux estranges régions,
> Qu'il fait bon pour les légions;
> C'est dans ces terres barbares
> Que, faisant guerre, nous pouvions
> Soûler nos courages avares.
>
> (Act III, p. 65, chorus of soldiers)

At the time when *Porcie* was published, a revolt in the Low Countries (August, 1566), followed by the Duke of Alva's appointment as Spanish commander there (December, 1566) and his passage through France with an army in the summer of 1567, had already drawn the attention of France to the Low Countries, so that Admiral Coligny's scheme was in the air, although he was not able to begin its realization until after 1570.

After this brief appearance in *Porcie*, the theme of foreign war as a means of preventing civil war now reappears in slightly expanded form in a soldiers' chorus in *Marc-Antoine*, coinciding with Anjou's use of the argument to support his own inglorious campaign in the Low Countries. Moreover, Garnier refers to Anjou's expedition in the dedication of the first (1579) edition of *La Troade*. It was probably less from any attachment to Anjou's cause, than from weariness with civil war, and willingness to lend support to any plan which offered a possibility of bringing it to an end.

---

[1] Cf. J. H. Mariéjol, *La Réforme et La Ligue*, p. 200.

In the year after the appearance of *Marc-Antoine* came *La Troade* (1579). Between the publication of the two plays came the agitated spring and summer of 1578 when, though nominally no war was in progress after the peace of Bergerac (September, 1577), the provinces, especially in the south, suffered the depredations of the armies of both sides; many horrific stories were recounted of the licentiousness and brutality of these bands of marauding soldiers. As usual, there is a lack of certain information as to date of composition, but it is tempting to think that these events gave special impetus to Garnier, who describes in *La Troade* not so much the horror of war itself, but the senseless continuation of hostilities after a war has been won. And just as troops from the two armies were causing distress to both sides, so Garnier emphasizes the common suffering and loss, in a dialogue between Hécube and Cassandre (Act I, 355–80) which contains lines such as:

> HÉCUBE: Nos peuples sont destruits.
> CASSANDRE: Leurs peuples sont ainsi.
> (367)

Garnier himself, in his dedication to Renaud de Beauve, suggests that the relevance of the play is as a consolation to the French; from this Trojan ruin sprang eventually the great French monarchy: similarly the present turmoil and agony of France may not be the end of the story.[1] It is difficult not to feel that this is a purely 'external' message, added afterwards to make an elegant preface; what comes across most clearly and insistently in *La Troade* is the misery and suffering, and there is no consciousness *within* the play that this is not the final and utter destruction of Troy:

> Le destin de Priam ne semble lamentable,
> Le destin de Priam ne luy est miserable,

[1] This is not the first time that Garnier has imitated Ronsard in attributing a Trojan ancestor to the French; he had already exploited the theme in one of the sonnets for the *Tombeau* of Charles IX, where he refers to the French king as:

> un nepveu d'Hector,
> Dont l'honneur court plus grand que d'Hector son ancestre.
> (Lebègue II, p. 239).

Priam est bien-heureux, qui, bornant son ennuy,
Vieil a veu trebucher son royaume avec luy.

O bien-heureux celuy qui, mourant en la guerre,
De soy-mesme heritier ne laisse rien sur terre:
Ains voit tout consommer devant que de mourir,
Et avecque sa mort toute chose perir!
(*La Troade*, Act I, 261–4, 269–72, Hécube)

By the time *Antigone* (1580) appeared, the seventh civil war
(the 'guerre des amoureux') had started. We find in this play
the repetition of some earlier themes, such as the description of
how both sides suffer in war (this comes in a chorus in Act III,
1456–1515, which Garnier had adapted from one in the first act
of Seneca's *Oedipus* describing Thebes struck by plague), and,
as in *Marc-Antoine*, the view of foreign war as a lesser evil
than civil war (Act II, 784–93 and 862–89). As though testing
this strategy, Anjou was still pursuing his futile plans; he had
returned in January, 1579 from his first expedition, and was
preparing another; he was to go again in 1581, and continue his
hopeless quest of a crown until by the stupid and ignoble blunder
of the 'French fury' at Antwerp in January, 1583 he ruined his
chances for ever.

Another kind of involvement with foreign countries also
occurs in *Antigone*. Polynice is criticized for bringing foreign
troops with him to intervene in a domestic quarrel (e.g. Act II,
805). French Protestants frequently appealed for help to Protestants in England, Germany or Scandinavia; the assembly of
Millau had made such an appeal in August, 1574; the *Reveille-*
matin of 1573–4 calls for a league of Protestant powers in
Europe to defend the Huguenots; an appeal to the English and
the Swiss can be found in *Le Tocsin contre les massacreurs* of 1577.
A foreign army had crossed the Meuse in January, 1576, and
in the spring of 1580 the Prince de Condé went to Germany to
try to raise another army. In short, foreign intervention was a
constant threat, and Garnier in his references to it is perhaps
criticising the Protestants who have so often invoked aid from
outside France.

Twice in this play there occurs a theme which has an odd but probably fortuitous relevance to the current phase of the wars. The Messenger (Act II, 540–7) and Jocaste (Act II, 578–9) both put forward the idea that the armies are less eager for war than the generals; these are Jocaste's words:

> Les camps vont lentement, mais les deux Capitaines
> Ont pour se rencontrer les demarches soudaines.

This has a curious aptness in 1580: some episodes in the religious wars had started more or less spontaneously, but the 'guerre des amoureux' seemed to have been started quite arbitrarily by Henri de Navarre, with so little reason that, as its nickname shows, people attributed its origin to the indignation provoked at Nérac (where Navarre held court) by Henri III's malicious gossip about the love affairs of Henri de Navarre and his queen. However, the chronology hardly allows us to link the 'guerre des amoureux', which began with Henri de Navarre's four-day siege of Cahors late in May, 1580, with *Antigone*, which must have been completed by then.

In her long speech to her sons in Act II of *Antigone*, Jocaste points out the particular folly of civil war when one side is led by the claimant to the throne, who is thus destroying what he hopes to win. This could be applied to Henri de Navarre, second in succession to the throne (who must have been struck by similar considerations seven years later, when after his victory at Coutras in October, 1587 he refrained from marching on Paris); it could also apply to Anjou, the heir presumptive, who as early as the fifth civil war had fought against the king. This does not mean that Polynice 'is' Henri de Navarre or François de Valois; but the situation has a certain similarity and Jocaste's words bring this out, partly by their very general nature:

> C'est la ville, mon fils, où Dieu vous a fait naistre,
> Et où vous desirez l'unique seigneur estre.
> Quelle bouillante rage et quel forcenement
> Vous espoind de vouloir destruire en un moment
> Vostre propre Royaume, et le voulant conquerre
> Le faire saccager par des hommes de guerre?
>
> (*Antigone*, Act II, 810–15)

These lines contain nothing to tie the passage down to Thebes, and a sixteenth-century reader or playgoer would therefore be free to make his own analogies.

Lastly, in *Antigone* Garnier deals with one really controversial question: whether or not a subject ought to obey an immoral edict. If we assume that Antigone is in the right (and we must, as she embodies 'la piété'), the answer he gives is a Protestant one:

> D'une ordonnance injuste il ne faut tenir compte.
>
> (*Antigone*, Act ɪv, 1552)

This agrees with Théodore de Bèze's opinion.[1] Garnier seems, however, to make an affort to counter this bold position by stressing also the virtue of obedience:

> *Mortels, nous n'avons rien*
> *Sur ce rond terrien,*
> *Qui tant nous soit utile*
> *Que d'observer les loix,*
> *Sous qui les justes Rois*
> *Gouvernent une ville.*
>
> (Act ɪv, 2092–7)

The requirements of the fable may force Garnier to defend civil disobedience, but he also includes a word on behalf of law and order.

Garnier's last two plays came at a time when Henri III's prestige was continuing to decline. Pamphleteers continued to stir up hatred against him and his government.[2] The breakdown of negotiations for the marriage of Anjou to Elizabeth of England, the defeat of Strozzi and the French fleet off the Azores by the Marquis of Santa-Cruz, were blows to national pride.

Garnier seems to be trying to remedy this low state of national self-respect in *Bradamante* (1582), by praising France and stressing her world-wide renown. France is the home of courage, military prowess, wealth, elegance and grace:

> la douceur et l'amour,

---

[1] See *Du Droit des magistrats* (*s.l.*, 1574) p. 723. One might add that if Catholics did not yet voice this opinion, it was because in their view the edicts disobeyed by the Protestants were not immoral and the question did not arise.

[2] E.g. Nicolas Barnaud (?), *Le Cabinet du Roy de France* (*s.l.*, 1581).

La richesse et l'honneur font à Paris séjour.

Such is the impression formed by the Bulgarian ambassadors
(Act v, 1551–2), expressed in lines that recapture the tone of
Marot's 'Dieu gard à la court'.

We notice in *Bradamante*, for the first time, the expression of
a religious conception of kingship, in Charlemagne's lines at the
beginning of the play. This was a controversial topic; supporters
of the monarchy often voiced the opinion that kingship sprang
from God (this might or might not be extended to the extreme
position of the 'Divine Right' theory), while Protestants and
malcontents were more inclined to say that power was originally
vested in the monarch by the people. (Ultra-Catholics and Protestants reversed their positions on this subject, and the related
one of tyrannicide, after the death of Anjou in 1584, when Henri
de Navarre became heir-presumptive to the throne.) Without
going into the intricacies of political theory, it is sufficient here
to point out that the opinion which Garnier puts into the mouth
of a king of France is one which involves respect for the monarch,
and also a certain humility on the part of the monarch. This same
blend of pride and humility can be seen in the words of Henri III
to the Estates General of 1588, expressing the same idea: 'Je
suis vostre Roy donné de Dieu et suis seul qui le puis veritable-
ment et légitimement dire; c'est pourquoi je ne veux estre en
ceste monarchie que ce que j'y suis, n'y pouvant souhaitter aussi
plus d'honneur ou plus d'authorité.'[1] It is noteworthy too that
Charlemagne is a good king; this till now has been a rare event in
Garnier's plays, but here we have not only the wise, magnani-
mous Charlemagne, constantly concerned with the welfare of his
subjects, but also young Roger promising the Bulgarian ambassadors that he will be a good king:

> Soyez-moy bons sujets, je vous seray bon prince.
> Je maintiendray le peuple en une heureuse paix,
> Faisant justice droicte à bons et à mauvais;
> Je me consacre à vous, et promets vous defendre
> Contre tous ennemis qui voudront vous offendre.
>
> (Act v, 1746–50)

---

[1] J. H. Mariéjol, *La Réforme et la Ligue*, p. 281.

Without saying that Roger 'is' Henri III, we can surmise that this situation—the young man whose main distinction is military prowess, elected to the throne of a distant country—would recall, to contemporary readers and spectators, Henri's election to the throne of Poland nine years earlier, when he too had sworn to protect his subjects, even to the extent of promising religious toleration ('Jurabis, aut non regnabis' had been the firm Polish refrain at every sign of reluctance to make such binding promises); so that this element of the play might be interpreted as a discreet tribute to Henri III.

We noticed that *La Troade*, which appeared after the sixth civil war, contained a bleak picture of the aftermath of war; *Bradamante* also appeared, and was probably composed, in a period of nominal peace, between the end of the seventh war (Peace of Fleix, November, 1580) and the beginning of the 'War of the three Henrys' after the resurgence of the Ligue in 1585; appropriately, it contains a discussion of the work of reconstruction which must follow war, and a picture of the moral chaos into which war has thrown the nation (Act I, scene ii).

When we come to the last play, *Les Juifves* (1583), we find Garnier again dealing with a topical question, that of rebellion. This time his answer is unequivocally on the side of established law and order. Sédécie is a pitiable figure; in many ways he is a good king, god-fearing, with a lofty conception of royal honour and duty, and an anguished concern for his people; but he is in the wrong, because as he and Amital freely admit, he has rebelled against his lawful overlord, Nabuchodonosor. Nabuchodonosor is a cruel and ungodly tyrant; but no-one in the play questions his right to punish Sédécie's rebellion.[1] Thus Garnier here puts the case for monarchy, even to the point of demanding a virtuous subject's obedience to an evil king. In his attitude to monarchy as it emerges in this play we also see a further statement of the religious concept which first appeared in *Bradamante*; even Nabuchodonosor, because he is a king, is:

> Le temple, la vertu, la semblance de Dieu.
>
> (Act IV, 1466. Sédécie)

[1] Further discussion of this point will be found in chapters 6 and 7.

Religious considerations also appear for the first time in Garnier's statement of the relevance of his play; in the dedication to the king's favourite, Joyeuse, he says that the tragedy deals with: 'les souspirables calamitez d'un peuple, qui a comme nous abandonné son Dieu'.

If we now look briefly at Garnier's career, we shall find support for the line that seems to emerge from his plays. He was a crown officer, but had little direct contact with the king, as he spent most of his life in the provinces and was never a courtier. Therefore, although he was indebted to the crown, and was a loyal servant to the house of Valois, he was not a flatterer (except in some conventionally fulsome dedications and in his *vers de circonstance*), and allowed a certain amount of criticism to show in his plays. But if we compare his first two plays with his last two, we notice a distinct change of tone. In *Porcie*, eloquent expression is given to the ideals of the republican party in Rome, and if tyrannicide is finally disavowed, it is on grounds of expediency, not principle. In *Les Juifves*, on the other hand, Garnier shows an evil, arrogant and bloodthirsty king, but nowhere in the play is there any suggestion that the way to deal with such a king is to assassinate him; the only courses open to the Jews are to beg for mercy and, when this is refused, to suffer with fortitude. Thus Garnier omits any hint of republican sentiment or approval of tyrannicide, as though being careful to avoid anything which might tend to weaken the already precarious position of Henri III. In both *Les Juifves* and *Bradamante* Garnier stresses the sanctity of kingship, even of Nabuchodonosor's kingship, and after an array of strutting princelings and conquerors (Jules-César, Octave, Pyrrhe, Créon), we suddenly have three good kings: Charlemagne, Roger and Sédécie (a good king though a bad vassal).

This change of emphasis can be explained as the loyalty of a crown servant, rallying to the cause of French monarchy. Another change is less easy to account for: why did Garnier in 1589, towards the end of his life, become a member of the Ligue?

Garnier's friends and patrons include men like Guy du Faur de Pibrac, who, with Michel de l'Hospital, formed the nucleus of the first generation of *politiques* (L'Hospital's disgrace in 1568 silenced this voice for peace and tolerance). Arée's speech in *Porcie* on the need for peace, in a central position in Act iii, is very close in theme and tone to some of L'Hospital's speeches and writings. Nothing could be more different from the peace-loving, humane, tolerant and intensely patriotic views of Michel de l'Hospital and his friends than the belligerent, bigoted Ligue, ready to hand France over to Spain rather than allow a Pro-testant king to accede to the French throne to which he was the legitimate heir.

There are several possible explanations for this action of Garnier's. He may have acted under compulsion, as many others did (and we know that by the following year he had already left the Ligue again). He may have been shocked into opposition by Henri III's 'execution' (as Henri probably regarded it) of the Duc de Guise in 1588. Or Henri III's own assassination, leaving Henri de Navarre as claimant to the throne, may have found Garnier unwilling, as an orthodox Catholic, to accept a Pro-testant king. (Henri III was only thirty-seven when he was killed; Garnier might have been hoping that there would yet be a Catholic heir to the throne—he was still uttering pious wishes to this effect in the preface to the 1585 edition of the plays, dedicated to Henri III).

But might not Garnier's choice of the Ligue be a logical continuation of the trend we have seen in his plays? The belief in the divine source of royalty, which we have seen in *Bradamante* and *Les Juifves*, might lead him to accept Henri de Navarre as the natural successor, or on the contrary might make him reluctant to accept a heretic as rightful heir to the throne of the Most Christian King. If moral scruples of this kind led him to join the Ligue, it is not surprising that he left it again within a year. Its leaders were not guided by ideals or moral principles.

All in all, the aspects of the political life of France to which Garnier seems to refer in his plays, and the tenor of the whole work, show him as a peace-loving man, anxious to see the end of the bitter, futile struggle which is dragging France to ruin; as the position of French monarchy deteriorates, he presents a more respectful attitude towards monarchy in his plays; and the religious conception of kingship which is evident in his last two plays may be the clue to his brief adherence to the ultra-Catholic Ligue, even though some Ligue propagandists found it expedient to take over discarded Protestant views on the popular origin of monarchy and the legality of tyrannicide.

4

THE KING AND KINGSHIP

In previous chapters I have stated the case for trying a political approach to Garnier and suggested, in chapter 3, that his plays reflect to some extent the events and concerns of the civil wars. This does not mean that they are *pièces à clé*, bearing a close relationship to specific events and people, but that in his choice of subjects and in his treatment of those subjects, Garnier was influenced by the political background of his time.

In this chapter and the two following, I shall analyse Garnier's political views and ideas, as they emerge from his writings, and compare them to the writings of expressly political writers (whether these are authors of theory, propaganda or polemics) in an attempt to determine Garnier's political position.

Before this analysis can be started, the question arises of how one decides what Garnier's views are. R. M. Griffiths, in a criticism of Kurt Willner's thesis *Montchrestiens Tragödien und die stoische Lebensweisheit* (Berlin, 1932), has commented on the fallacy of supposing that a sixteenth-century dramatist has a 'message' which can be determined from an examination of the *sententiæ* in his plays.[1] Dr Griffiths observes that because the *sententiæ* are ornamental, often derivative, and contradictory (especially when used in stichomythia), they cannot be taken as representing the *Weltanschauung* of the author, and in Montchrestien, at least, they do not form any coherent system of thought.

In spite of this I think that one can, with caution, form a reasonable hypothesis as to the views held by Garnier on political topics (or, to be scrupulous, the views which he was willing to

[1] R. M. Griffiths, 'Les sentences et le "but moral" dans les tragédies de Montchrestien', in *R.S.H.*, no. 105 (1962) p. 5.

appear to hold—and the possible discrepancy is not important to my purpose) from an examination of his writings.

In arriving at such a hypothesis, I have been guided by the following considerations: firstly, I have felt free to use Garnier's tragi-comedy, *Bradamante*, as well as his prefaces and non-dramatic poetry, when this material helped to illuminate Garnier's ideas; this seemed justifiable since, if he really has any political preoccupations, there is no reason to suppose that the text of the tragedies forms a water-tight compartment in which they are all contained.

Secondly, within the plays I am of course not confining myself to *sententiæ*. This means that some of the difficulties pointed out by R. M. Griffiths disappear automatically. It is true that the *sententiæ* taken alone are often contradictory. But it is possible to determine from context which of the *sententiæ* the author intends us to accept and which are 'wrong' within the framework of a certain situation. Among Garnier's plays, some have as their general theme a political topic (e.g. *La Troade*, where the theme is the aftermath of war), others a political problem (e.g. *Porcie*, the problem of tyrannicide). In every play which has a political problem as its general theme, a solution to the problem is offered. This solution may be implicit in the ending of the play, or there may be an explicit judgment as in *Antigone*; in this play there is obviously a certain amount of right on both sides, and the questions involved (whether it is wrong to disobey an immoral edict, and whether a king is bound by his own laws) were much debated in the sixteenth century. The audience therefore might be unable to decide who, if anyone, was to blame in the play. The answer is given by the chorus:

> Créon eut vrayment tort
>
> (Act iv, 2146)

Not that the chorus, in this or any other play, can always be taken either as being the mouthpiece of the author or as putting into words the presumed (or desired) reaction of the audience. But in the passage from which I have just quoted, the chorus of Thebans speak in a tone of such firm, considered judgment that we are impelled to think that they are offering us Garnier's own views: Créon, for all his good intentions, erred in his inflexibility, and in not taking into account Antigone's royal blood, as well as in his initial fault of promulgating an ungodly edict. We are all the more willing to accept the verdict of the chorus because they also point out the good intentions on Créon's part:

> Il pense tesmoigner
> Pour les siens n'espargner
> Qu'il fait justice egale.
>
> (Act IV, 2149–51)

But the problems involved in the plays would not be worth solving if there was not a certain amount of weight on both sides, and so the 'wrong' side is usually presented in fairly vigorous terms, giving rise to the disputes in *sententiæ* which R. M. Griffiths sees as a source of contradiction and confusion to anyone looking for a positive 'message' in the plays. They need not be, since it is usually quite clear which side the audience is intended to agree with. Let us look, for example, at the lengthy dispute (part of which is in *sententiæ*) between Pyrrhe and Agamemnon in Act III of *La Troade*. Some of their *sententiæ* are directly contradictory, as:

PYRRHE: *Il n'est point defendu par les loix de la guerre*
De tuer les haineux de sa natale terre.
AGAMEMNON: *L'honneur et le devoir defendent maintesfois*
De faire ce qui n'est defendu par les loix.
PYRRHE: *Ce qui plaist au vaincueur est loisible de faire.*
AGAMEMNON: *D'autant qu'il peut beaucoup, d'autant luy doit moins*
plaire.

> (*La Troade*, Act III, 1481–6)

Throughout the argument, Pyrrhe is given lines quite as forceful as those of Agamemnon, he puts his case just as cogently, and he is less ready to descend from argument to irrelevant abuse, as Agamemnon does:

> Mais tu n'es qu'un bastard, encor quand tu fus fait
> Ton engendreur Achil' n'estoit homme parfait.
>
> (1495–6; see also 1490, 1492, 1501)

That Agamemnon stoops to this level of personal insult might give the impression that his case is the weaker of the two; an impression which seems confirmed by the fact that Pyrrhe wins: that is, when he and Agamemnon submit their quarrel to Calchas's judgment, the decision is in favour of Pyrrhe. But in spite of all this, there is clearly no doubt as to where Garnier's sympathies lie, and which of the two is to be regarded as in the right. It is Agamemnon. Two things make this clear. Firstly, the whole play deals with the aftermath of war, with the sufferings common to both sides, and with the terrible way in which hatred, fear and killing continue after the end of a war. Therefore Agamemnon, with his recognition of the horrors of war and concern to put an end to destruction and terror, is expressing ideas in keeping with the theme of the play and is in fact putting forward the only possible 'solution' or 'moral' when he says:

> *Pyrrhe, c'est peu de vaincre, il faut considerer*
> *Ce qu'un vainqueur doit faire, un vaincu endurer.*
>
> (Act III, 1403–4)

Patience on the part of the defeated, restraint and humanity on the part of the conqueror: these are the only attitudes which can make the disaster bearable. Agamemnon is expressing an idea which is central to the play. The second reason for one's conviction that Agamemnon is right lies in the style of his speeches, particularly of the long speech, lines 1397–1440, part of which runs as follows:

> Aussi le Ciel j'atteste, et le throsne des Dieux
> Qu'oncques je n'eus vouloir d'abatre, furieux,
> Les Pergames de Troye, et de mettre à l'espee
> Par un sac inhumain cette terre occupee.
> Sans plus je desirois voir leur coeur endurci
> Contraint à demander de leur faute merci:
> Mais du soldat ne peut l'outrageuse insolence
> Tellement se domter qu'il n'use de licence,
> Quand la nuict, la victoire, et le courroux luy ont
> Acharné le courage, et mis l'audace au front.
>   Donc ce qui est resté de sa rage, demeure:
> C'est assez, je ne veux qu'aucun de sang froid meure:

Je ne le veux souffrir, endurer je ne doy
Qu'à mes yeux on esgorge une fille de Roy,
Qu'on plonge le cousteau dans ses entrailles tendres,
Et de son chaste sang on arrose des cendres.

(Act III, 1419–34)

The language of this speech is strongly emotive; various techniques are used to make it so and the result is that the reader's (or hearer's) sympathies are won and he accepts Agamemnon's point of view as 'right' because he is moved by its presentation.[1] Thus the use of *sententiæ* even in disputes does not necessarily prevent a very clear 'message' from coming through; and when this message is achieved by the choice of persuasive language which captures the reader's sympathy, it is clear that we are dealing with a writer who controls very carefully the emotional and intellectual responses of his audience.[2]

However, there are some disputes and debates where we are less sure of the answer. Neither character seems to be decisively in the right, and even if the emotional colouring is all on one side, we may feel that the other side is supported by common sense and by practical considerations. Therefore, in analysing Garnier's political views my third consideration has been that an argument that seems to have two equally valid sides, an unresolved dispute, or a topic discussed several times with varying degrees of cogency or passion on one side or the other, may indicate a problem which Garnier himself found insoluble, or where all his sympathies lay with one side, and all his sense of the expedient with the other. An example of this is the recurring *clémence/rigueur* debate, which will be discussed in detail later in chapter 6.

After these preliminary remarks, I can now begin the analysis

---

[1] Further discussion of Garnier's methods of giving emotional colouring to a theme or speech, and of 'loading' an apparently straightforward dialogue or *récit*, will be found in chapter 7.

[2] It is also worth noting that at least one sixteenth-century dramatic theorist was quite explicit about the function of the *sententiæ* in tragedy: 'Sententiae [. . .] sunt enim quasi columnae aut pilae quaedam totius fabricae illius [. . .] quibus tota tragoedia est fulcienda'. J.–C. Scaliger, *Poetices libri septem* (Lyon, 1561) *Lib.* III, *cap.* xcvii.

of the political views expressed by Garnier, and compare them with those of sixteenth-century political writers.

The political questions most frequently and hotly debated in the sixteenth century centred on the theme of monarchy—what was the origin of monarchy? how did it compare in merit with other forms of state? how should a king be educated, how choose his counsellors? what was the proper relationship between him and his people, should he rule by fear or affection? in what did the royal prerogative consist and what limits were there upon the king's freedom of action? was he answerable to his subjects, to God or only to himself? These are some of the questions which were frequently, and very relevantly, debated under the last Valois kings, when the very existence of the French monarchy was at times in danger and when opposing factions tended to claim that whatever they did—even if it was kidnapping the king—they were acting in the best interests of the crown, and defending the true principles of monarchy.

Writings on this subject took various forms; many works were in the form of an 'Institution du roi'—which was bound to include ideas on the theory of kingship and the nature of a good king, since the writer had to make plain what he was hoping to achieve by his educational plan.[1] Others were compilations of the opinions of ancient writers on the subject.[2] Some were treatises outlining the ideal prince.[3] Others were historical, with or without some biassed reference to contemporary problems.[4]

Quite apart from the very numerous references to kingship in his plays, Garnier produced one separate piece of writing on the subject of monarchy: his *Hymne de la monarchie* (Lebègue II,

---

[1] See bibliography for titles of such works by Symphorien Champier, Guillaume Budé, Claude d'Espence, J. Antoine de Baïf.

[2] E.g. F. de Saint Thomas, *La Vraye forme de bien et heureusement regir, et gouverner un royaume ou Monarchie: ensemble le vray office d'un bon Prince* (Lyon, 1569).

[3] E.g. J. Heluïs de Thillard, *Le Miroüer du prince chretien* (Paris, 1566); Claude Gousté, *Traicté de la puissance et authorité des roys* (*s.l.*, 1561).

[4] E.g. François Hotman, *Franco-Gallia* (Geneva, 1573); Louis Le Roy, *Consideration sur l'histoire françoise, et l'universelle de ce temps* (Paris, 1567); François de Belleforest, *Les Grandes annales, et histoire generale de France, des la venue des Francs en Gaule, jusques au regne du roy tres-Chrestien Henry III* (Paris, 1579).

pp. 216–32), published in 1567. This is a long poem (532 lines) dealing with various aspects of the subject, and I propose to examine it in detail partly because it is not much read, partly because when critics do comment on it, they often give what seems to me a misleading impression of it. The poem is dedicated to Guy du Faur de Pibrac, and opens with sixteen lines of praise for Pibrac's loyal service to the French crown. The rest falls into the following divisions:

1. lines 17–38: a description (imitated from Lucretius) of the brutish life of primitive man—a non-social, fearful, cannibalistic and furry creature ('plus velus qu'un Ours', a detail which is not to be found in Lucretius), lacking any rule of law or reason, any ties of family or marriage, guided only by his passions.

2. lines 39–106: a piece of myth-making (modelled in part on the myth of Astrée) describing Monarchy as a force of order in the universe. Having exercised this ordering faculty on creation in general (the separation of the elements), Monarchy directed her attention to man, taught him husbandry, city-building and the social virtues, instituted marriage and enabled man to discover his immortal soul. The gods Apollo, Bacchus and Hermes and the goddess Pallas were all monarchs on earth before being deified. Thus Monarchy is supreme in heaven and on earth.

3. lines 107–43: the poet compares monarchy with other forms of state (democracy and aristocracy) and declares that they are inferior to monarchy; he comments on the good fortune of the peoples of the Assyrian, Medean and Persian empires in being under monarchic rule.

4. lines 144–212: Monarchy is the 'natural' order: the lion, eagle and whale are 'king' in the three parts of the animal kingdom. Bees are a perfect example of a monarchic state—a lengthy description is given, stressing their good organization and devotion to their 'king'.

5. lines 213–88: a possible objection is that a prince often, in fact almost always, becomes a tyrant. Garnier gives several answers to this: firstly that every good thing can be abused and turned to evil ends; secondly that an aristocracy can also turn to tyranny, and various examples are given from Persian, Spartan and Roman history of this multiple tyranny; thirdly, there is

more chance of one man being good than several; and fourthly, where there are several in command they are bound to quarrel, and destroy the state with their dissensions.

6. lines 289–320: a second objection: that liberty is important and precious. To answer this, Garnier first distinguishes between licence and liberty (his description of licence is reminiscent of the earlier passage on primitive man) and says that true liberty, the right to behave well and serve one's country, flourishes under monarchic rule; furthermore, he claims that even if there is slavery under a prince's rule, there is more under the rule of several (virtually a repetition of the second answer to the previous objection).

7. lines 321–438: a third possible objection: that democracy might work, and has worked for the most famous cities of the past. The first answer to this is merely a contemptuous dismissal of the idea, followed by a lengthy image of a pilotless ship where all the crew tries to command and the result is confusion and final disaster. The second answer cites some specific disadvantages of the great democracies of the past, particularly their ingratitude to those who had served them well. Thirdly, the poet describes the sorry situation that arises when democratic rule is exploited by ambitious men, as happened in Rome.

8. lines 439–94: but Rome's greatness started under the rule of kings, and when she returned to single rule, with Augustus, there was a Golden Age of peace, and the arts flourished, especially poetry.

9. lines 495–532: the poem ends with an allegorical description of the goddess Monarchy throned in royal splendour, surrounded by her supporters Loyauté, Force, Prudence, Obeissance, Justice and Clemence, and with a prayer to her to prosper the house of Valois and the young Charles IX.

From this summary of the poem, it can be seen that Garnier has combined various approaches to the subject; there is the historical, as when he refers to the succession of empires and to many incidents in Greek and Roman history; on the theoretical and philosophical side, there is the theory that monarchy is 'natural', and the traditional discussion of the three forms of state—monarchy, aristocracy and democracy; there are also typical rhetorical techniques, personification, allegory, the myth-element, the extended metaphor. In these respects the poem makes no startling contribution to the subject.

But the *Hymne* has been described as a sort of manifesto, a testimony of Garnier's complete loyalty to the crown, his fervent belief in monarchy.[1] Can the poem support this interpretation? I find the *Hymne* disturbing, from various points of view. First, it is a bad poem. This of course proves nothing about Garnier's attitude to the content, but the particular ways in which it is bad are interesting and suggestive. There is little here that is worthy of the poet of 'Pauvres filles de Sion' or the elegy on the death of Ronsard. True, the *Hymne* is an early work, but it was only in the following year that *Porcie* appeared, and there are many passages in that (the moving lament at the end of the play, the arrogant debate of the Triumvirs) to prove that Garnier is already skilled in handling language and controlling his effects. Very occasionally in the *Hymne* there is a line with the sonority one associates with Garnier:

> Composa le repos de ce monde indonté . . .
>
> (54)

or a brief flash of his visual imagination:

> Sur la cave épesseur des tristes corcelés
> L'Areigne industrieuse étendit ses filés . . .
>
> (461–2)[2]

But as a whole the poem is dispiritingly pompous and mediocre. It is disconcerting to find that the passage which, in the middle of this arid composition, suddenly reminds us that we are, after all, reading the work of a good poet, has almost no direct bearing on the subject of monarchy. Garnier begins the passage about the

---

[1] E.g. by M.–M. Mouflard who refers to it as a 'profession de foi politique' (*Robert Garnier*, vol. I, p. 148).
[2] Cf. a passage in *Marc-Antoine* (Act III, p. 211):

> Sa masse domteresse aux solives pendoit;
> Son arc comme jadis encordé ne tendoit;
> Sur ses flèches filoit la mesnagère araigne,
> Et son dur vestement estoit percé de teigne.

bees almost apologetically:

> Lairay-je en ce propos, de silence pressé
>
> (153)

It is as though he is aware that the theme is a hackneyed one; but he warms to the subject and gives some entertaining details about the highly organized society of the bees:

> Vous en verrés les uns, errant sans faire bruit,
> A la garde du camp vueiller toute la nuit.
> Puis, si tost que le jour a la terre alumée,
> Bourdonner par troys fois pour éveiller l'armée.
>
> (181–4)

The whole passage ends by praising the bees for their devotion to their prince in a tribute which, even if the subject is slightly absurd, is worthy of its author for its graceful movement, rich assonances and delicate feeling:

> Pour une telle amour puissiés-vous en tout tems
> Eprouver la douceur d'un éternel printems:
> En tout tems puissiés-vous, Abeilles innocentes,
> Moissonner les odeurs des fleurettes naissantes,
> Et du suc doucereus qui s'ecoule du ciel,
> Confire en vos maisons de la cire et du miel.
> Les frelons outrageus, ny les Guespes cruelles
> N'epinssonnent jamais vos poitrines fidelles:
> Jamais les vents enflés, ny les froids de l'yver,
> Sur vos jaunes bournaus ne puissent arriver.
>
> (201–10)

This has nothing to do with political theory or history, it is merely a delightful decorative flourish. It is strange that Garnier's most successful verse in this poem should be irrelevant to the subject of the poem. The fact is not in itself sufficient evidence for us to conclude that Garnier found the subject of monarchy uninteresting, or the attitude to it presented in this poem unsatisfactory; but the poem contains several other pointers in the same direction. One is the extreme abstractness of the writing (and Garnier is noted for the physical quality of his language); thus although 'Monarchie' is personified, she has no face, no physical characteristics at all, only a band of equally faceless, allegorical courtiers; and in this lengthy panegyric of monarchy,

Garnier never mentions a good king by name, except Augustus who of course was not strictly speaking a king at all; and in enumerating the benefits that Rome enjoyed under Augustus's rule, he is careless or tactless enough to mention (189–95) the works of Ovid—who was banished by that same emperor.

Another disturbing feature is the speciousness of the arguments employed. Garnier had a lawyer's ability to marshal arguments and to handle debate, and this is seen clearly in the plays, both in the long speeches and the clashes of stichomythic rejoinder. It is quite invisible here. To objections that bad things happen under monarchic rule he can only offer the rather helpless reply that they also happen under other forms of government (213 ff.). Other arguments are even more specious; thus he says monarchy is better than aristocracy because:

> tout chacun sçait bien
> Qu'on rencontre plutost un seul homme de bien
> Qu'une grand'troupe ensemble, et qu'il est difficille
> Qu'en tel nombre ne sont la plus part inutile.
>
> (273–6)

Since he implies that good men are rarer than bad, he might just as well argue that a single ruler is more likely to be bad than good, whereas a 'grand'troupe' may contain at least some good men. In any case, Garnier here contradicts his previous admission (213–24) that princes more often than not become tyrants.

At other times he does not argue, he simply asserts. This is the technique he employs when dealing with democracy; first a scathing rhetorical question, heavily loaded with pejorative adjectives:

> Croyroit-on qu'un païs, du peuple gouverné,
> Se puisse jamais voir sagement ordonné?
> Et qu'au sot appetit d'une tourbe aveuglée
> Une grande Cité puisse estre bien reglée?
>
> (325–8)

Then the bald assertion that 'un maneuvre grossier' is incapable of handling affairs of state. Equally bald, and quite unconvincing,

is his second answer to the objection that monarchical rule
entails loss of liberty:

> Et bien que sous un Prince il y eust du servaige,
> Le regne de plusieurs en couve davantaige.
>
> (315–16)

If this argument is true, then, at best, Garnier is offering
monarchy as the least of several evils—and this negative merit
hardly justifies the allegorical glorification of monarchy elsewhere in the poem. If monarchy is only the best that can be
managed in an imperfect world, it does not seem to live up to
Garnier's invocation, 'ô puissante Déesse!' (439), 'ô suprême
Déesse!' (495).

Another curious characteristic of the poem is the way in which
the rhetorical colouring is distributed. Sometimes this results
in an objection being presented strongly, even though no strong
arguments will be produced to refute it. For example, here is
the passage in which Garnier introduces the objection that a
monarch may become a tyrant:

> Or peut-estre on dira qu'un Prince va souvent
> D'un Tyran débordé la nature ensuivant,
> Et qu'à peine voit-on que celuy qui maitrise
> Seul en une Cité les siens ne tyranise:
> Que delà sont venus tant de faits inhumains
> Aus Barbares, aus Grecs, et depuis aus Romains.
>
> (213–18)

(A catalogue of sixteen tyrants follows.) The use of 'souvent'
and 'à peine' suggests that it is rare for a prince *not* to become a
tyrant, while the words 'débordé', 'tyranise', 'inhumain' emphasize the idea of tyranny. This adds force to the objection, which
is not countered by any argument robust enough to cancel it.

Another point where the rhetoric seems to be working in the
wrong direction is in the passage beginning at line 137, where
Garnier celebrates the happy lot enjoyed by the subjects of the
Assyrian kings:

> Heureus cent et cent fois les peuples anciens
> Sugets aus volontés des Roys Assiriens,
> Qui, monarques premiers au giron de l'Asie,
> La regirent long-tems suivant leur fantaisie.

Here, the phrases 'sugets aus volontés' and 'suivant leur fantaisie' certainly suggest the capricious rule of a tyrant (cf. Créon at his most tyrannical: 'Telle est ma volonté' (*Antigone*, Act iv, 2034)). This implication is contrary to, and thus damages the force of, the explicit content of the passage, which is expressing envy of the subjects of these kings.

Thus the quality of the writing, the weakness of the arguments and the illogical distribution of rhetorical emphasis make this poem curiously unsatisfactory as a eulogy of monarchy. It certainly does not carry conviction as a political 'profession de foi'. If it is propaganda it is, for all its length, perfunctory.

One way of looking at it is to see it as a rhetorical exercise; the 'hymn' is a definite *genre* with its own rules, and Garnier follows the prescribed form (for instance, it was normal to end the *hymne* with a prayer, as Garnier does here). But though this conception of the poem may mean that strength or weakness of the arguments is unimportant, it makes the language of central importance, so that the indiscriminate use of rhetorical emphasis which disturbs the tone of the poem and makes its direction unclear appears even more strange.

A possible explanation suggests itself if we consider certain lines in *Porcie*, Garnier's first play, which may well have been already partly written when the *Hymne de la monarchie* was composed.

Porcie is the character in this play with whom we are asked to sympathize. She is the daughter of Cato, the wife of Brutus; from what we, the audience, know of the Portia of history (or the Portia of Plutarch) we expect her to be a fervent republican. There are certainly many fine lines in the play in praise of republicanism, praising the tyrannicides for their efforts on behalf of Roman liberty, criticizing the dead Caesar for his repressive rule, and showing by his own words that the next Caesar, Octavian, will be just as harsh and is indeed already gloating over his hold on Rome and his suppression of civic liberties. Yet Porcie herself changes her mind about the value of what her husband has done. Tyrannicide is useless, liberty an illusion. In killing Caesar, all that has been achieved is a multiplicity of tyrants where there was one before:

Nous tuasmes César pour n'avoir point de rois,
Mais au meurtre de luy nous en avons faict trois.

(Act II, p. 37)

Cf. *Hymne de la monarchie:*

Et bien que sous un Prince il y eust du servaige,
Le regne de plusieurs en couve davantaige.

(315–16)

In other words, the rule of one man, even a tyrant, is preferable
to anarchy or 'multiple tyranny'. This is not a defence of the
theory of monarchy, nor does it seem to embody any kind of
emotional conviction, but a coldly practical assessment. This
seems to provide a clue which would make sense of the *Hymne
de la monarchie.* Garnier's support of monarchy is not philosophical nor yet instinctive in origin; at this date, he does not even
suggest a Christian conception of the subject; monarchy is right
because it works and because a republican system which might
seem to offer more liberty for the individual in fact leads to
chaos and suffering. Appealing in principle, such a system is
condemned by its results.[1]

The *Hymne de la monarchie,* then, does not allow us to assume
that Garnier was an uncritical monarchist; it suggests, rather,
that he adopts a position (unusual for the sixteenth century) of
supporting the system simply because it is the best in practice,
without necessarily agreeing with the theoretical arguments
normally adduced in its favour. This makes it all the more
interesting to examine what he has to say in the plays on specific
topics connected with kingship, and to see how this compares
with other writers. In the *Hymne* there are already signs of
the wide range of Garnier's literary sympathies, and his
similarity, at various points, to a number of political thinkers
who may have little in common with each other. Thus the theme
that true liberty lies in obedience is to be found in the Catholic

[1] One of the few sixteenth-century writers to take such a pragmatic view of the
superiority of monarchy is the eccentric Raoul Spifame who in his *Dicaearchiae
Henrici regis Christianissimi progymnasmata* (*s.l.n.d.,* 1556?), a collection of 'edicts'
supposed to be issued by Henri II, says that monarchy is the best form of government because it offers the quickest way of getting things done (preamble to *Arrest*
19).

writer Guillaume des Autels (*Harengue au peuple françois contre la rebellion*, Paris, 1560), and later in the Protestant François Hotman's *Franco-Gallia* (1573) and in the *République* (1576) of Jean Bodin. The importance and worth of freedom is a subject dear to Michel de l'Hospital. The *topos* of the bees comes into French literature originally from Virgil (*Georgics*, IV) and is used by Alain Chartier in the *Quadrilogue invectif* of 1422; the same image of political organization and co-operation is used by a writer a generation older than Garnier, Gilles d'Aurigny, in his *Livre de police humaine* (Paris, 1544). The idea of monarchy as in some way the 'natural' form of government is very common among sixteenth-century writers: Le Roy and Bodin are two of its proponents.[1] The image of the ship badly governed in a storm, which Garnier uses in the *Hymne*, is also a commonplace one. The king is often compared to the captain of a ship, or her pilot, and we also find the comparison of a divided kingdom to a boat with a disagreeing crew; this image is used, for example, in a speech made by Michel de l'Hospital at the opening of the Paris Parlement in November, 1561: 'N'y a royaume qui puisse durer ne navire éviter le naufrage quand les ungs qui le conduisent font d'une sorte les aultres d'au contraire'.

A frequent theme in sixteenth-century writings on kingship is the definition of a king. In the work of jurists and others who approach the subject from a legal angle, the definition normally consists of a list of the 'marks of sovereignty', for example legislative authority, the administration of justice, power of life and death over subjects, the right to declare war and to levy taxes to pay for it, which are attributed to the king. The marks of sovereignty vary from writer to writer, according to whether the list is drawn up by a supporter of absolute monarchy or by one who advocates some limitations to royal prerogative.[2] The other way of defining a king is antithetically, by opposition to a

---

[1] Commenting on Le Roy's use of this doctrine, J. W. Allen adds rather obscurely: 'This notion was widely current in the sixteenth century, though it is not easy to say exactly what the notion was.' (*A history of political thought in the sixteenth century* (London, 1928) p. 379.)

[2] A typical list is given by Charles de Grassaille in *Regalium Franciae* . . . (Lyon, 1538).

tyrant. This method is defended by Louis Le Roy in *De l'Origine*
. . . *de l'art politique* (Paris, 1567), thus:

Laquelle maniere d'enseigner par contraires, est observee en plusieurs
disciplines, et est de merveilleuse efficace [. . .]. Car le bien ne peut
estre parfaittement entendu ny estimé, sinon en le conferant avec le mal,
ny le mal evité, et donté, sans l'ayde du bien cogneu.

(p. 14 recto–14 verso)

Le Roy is one of many writers who employ the technique of
'enseigner par contraires' to give a double picture of the good
and bad king.[1]

Garnier may be said to use both these techniques. The legists'
list of marks of sovereignty is a technical outline of the exact
content of the royal prerogative, and is often a mosaic of relics
of feudalism, and concepts drawn from Roman law. Garnier's
literary version of this can be seen in a speech in *La Troade*
where Andromaque describes the royal functions which Astyanax will never be able to fulfil, and in *Antigone* when Antigone
lists the kingly offices which Edipe has abandoned. Here, first, is
Andromaque:

> O mon fils, mon cher fils, verray-je point le jour
> Que, reparant l'honneur de ce natal sejour,
> Vous redressez les tours et les palais antiques
> Du flambant Ilion, les Pergames Troïques?
> Verray-je point le temps que nos peuples espars
> Vous r'assemblez, leur Roy, dedans nouveaux rempars,
> Que la gloire et le nom ressusciter je voye
> Par vos armes, mon fils, d'une nouvelle Troye?

(Act ii, 671–8)

The characteristics of kingship in this are that the king is the
guardian of his people's honour, and their leader in war, and that
it is his duty to restore the country after defeat. (In the corre-
sponding passage in Seneca, *Troades* 469–74, there is more stress

---

[1] Among others using the prince/tyrant antithesis are Jean Bodin in *Les VI livres
de la république* (Paris, 1576) Livre ii, Jean Heluïs de Thillard in *Le Mirouër du
prince chretien* (1566) and Nicolas Barnaud (?) in *Le Miroir des Francois* (1581).

on revenge and less on the work of restoring the shattered city.)

This is how Garnier's Antigone speaks to Edipe of the duties he has resigned:

> Je ne demande pas que vous vueillez encor
> Reprendre en vostre main le sceptre d'Agenor:
> Je ne demande pas que de loix salutaires
> Vous vueillez gouverner vos peuples volontaires;
> Et que vostre famille abysmee en malheur
> Vous vueillez redresser en son antique honneur:
> Je ne vous requiers pas que le dueil qui vous tue
> Vous vueillez despouiller de vostre ame abatue.
>
> (*Antigone*, Act I, 191–8)

The 'marks of sovereignty' here are three: the outward symbol of kingship ('le sceptre d'Agenor'); the function of law-giver; and the fact that the office of king is vested in one family.

Another statement of this kind comes in the dialogue of Charlemagne and Nymes in the first act of *Bradamante*:

CHARLEMAGNE: Nos peuples sont beaucoup par la guerre esclaircis,
Mais les vices au lieu sont beaucoup espessis.

NYMES: C'est l'office d'un Roy d'en purger sa contree:
Inutile est la Paix sans sa compagne Astree.
Vous devez en repos vos peuples maintenir,
Et de severes loix leurs offenses punir.

CHARLEMAGNE: Je veux recompenser un chacun de ses peines.

> (Act I, 159–65)

Here a moral function is attributed to the king, in his capacity of law-giver and judge. He is expected to keep his country 'en repos' and to hand out punishments and rewards.

All these points can be found in the writings of jurists and political and constitutional theorists. The first three (the king as guardian of his people's honour, as their leader in war and as restorer of the country after defeat) add up to something approaching the paternalistic view of kingship which is so common in sixteenth-century writers. We find it also in Garnier's last two plays. In *Les Juifves* we have Sédécie pleading for his people, who have erred only in being loyal to his transgression:

ce peuple sauvez, qui n'a fait autre mal
Sinon de se defendre et de m'estre loyal.

(Act IV, 1417–18)

In *Bradamante*, in addition to the lines just quoted, it can be seen throughout the play in Charlemagne's attitude to his subjects and his concern for their welfare.

That the king's main aim should be the *bien public* is the view expressed by Estienne Pasquier in the *Pourparler du prince* (first published in 1560).[1] Later, Jean de la Madeleyne, using images of the father of a family, a doctor, a ship's captain, also states that the king must put his people's interests first.[2] François de Saint Thomas is another writer who, following Homer, describes the king as the father and shepherd of the people, implying concern for welfare, protection and leadership.[3] The anonymous Huguenot author of the *Contrepoison* also expresses the view that the king is the *persona* of the state ('personne publique'), that he embodies 'le bien de son peuple' and is committed to their defence.[4] Like Garnier in *Antigone* (192) he mentions the sceptre as the outward symbol of majesty. The Huguenot attitude in this work is that the Huguenot wants neither absolutism nor anarchy, but king and constitution. La Madeleyne, Pasquier, Saint Thomas, the Huguenot writer of 1578, all of whom appear to have affinities with Garnier in their basic notion of kingship, are all moderates and constitutionalists, not uncritical devotees of monarchy.

In the quotation from *Bradamante* we saw the suggestion that the king ought also to set a moral example to his people and correct their vices. La Madeleyne requires of the king that he be a model of 'modestie et continence'.[5] Baïf informs Henri III that it is part of his duty to provide his subjects with a moral exemplar:

Fay qu'on aime le bien, et le mal se haïsse,

---

[1] Reprinted in *Recherches de la France* (Paris, 1660) p. 890 *ff.*

[2] *Discours de l'estat et office d'un bon roy, prince ou monarque* . . . (Paris, 1575), pp. 6–7.

[3] In *La Vraye forme de bien et heureusement regir* . . . (Lyon, 1569), p. 28; the same passage from Homer is quoted by Le Roy in *Exhortation aux François* . . . (Paris, 1570) pp. 65–66.

[4] *Advertissement sur le pourparlé, qu'on dit de paix, entre le Roy et ses rebelles. Avec son contrepoison* (anonymous), (Paris, 1568).

[5] J. de la Madeleyne, *op. cit.*, p. 72 *verso*.

Si cheris la vertu, si detestes le vice,
Aysêment le feras, bien né comme tu l'es:
Quel se monstre le ROY, tels se font les sugets.[1]

D'Albon takes this further and says that the king is superior to
ordinary men as men are superior to beasts, while Le Roy sees
the king not only as a paragon of virtue but as 'loy vivante'.[2] Le
Roy is a proponent of absolutism, and so is Claude d'Albon, the
latter because of his strong Catholic principles rather than on
theoretical or legal grounds; Garnier does not go as far as they
in his picture of the king as a moral leader.

Le Roy's phrase 'loy vivante' brings us to a large and intri-
cate problem: the question of the king and the law. In the passage already quoted from *Antigone*, it is apparent that legislation
is part of the royal prerogative, and that the good king is the
one who makes good laws ('salutaire' has been added by
Garnier to Seneca's text). Furthermore he has to impose this
law on a possibly refractory people ('peuple volontaire' (*Antigone*, 194), and compare 'les loix dont ils ne tiennent conte'
(*Antigone*, 1841) in Créon's definition of royal power). In
Bradamante the question arises whether the prince is bound by
his own edicts; Béatrix says he is, Aymon replies that it depends
on the subject of the edict:

BÉATRIX: *C'est chose malaisee, un Prince ne viole*
Les Edicts qu'il a faits, il maintient sa parole.

AYMON: Voire en chose publique, et qui est de grand poix:
Mais en chose privee on change quelquefois.

(Act II, 237–40)

Charlemagne does in fact observe his own edict, which had
established the strange terms on which Bradamante was to be
won in marriage; he has to, for the purposes of the plot, so that
one cannot draw any conclusions from this, but it is noteworthy
that Garnier does air the question in this sententious form. The
problem had arisen in an earlier play, when in *Antigone* Créon

---

[1] J. A. de Baïf, *Epistre au Roy* . . . (1575), p. 4 *recto*.
[2] Claude d'Albon, *De la Majesté royale* . . . (Lyon, 1575) p. 6 *recto*; Louis Le
Roy, *De l'Excellence du gouvernement royal* (Paris, 1575) p. 9 *verso*.

insists that he is bound by his own law (forbidding anyone to bury Polynice's body) and must punish Antigone for breaking it. Not only has he already promulgated this edict, but in Act IV, just before Antigone is brought in by the guards, he re-states it with a solemn oath, as though ritually binding himself to it:

> Je jure par le ciel qui ce monde environne,
> Par cet honoré sceptre, et par cette couronne,
> Que si aucun Thebain j'y voy contrevenir,
> Sans espoir de pardon je le feray punir,
> *Fust-il mon enfant propre. Une ordonnance est vaine,*
> *Si l'infracteur d'icelle est exempt de la peine.*
>
> (Act IV, 1736–41)

This speech is obviously placed here partly for dramatic effect, as almost immediately afterwards Antigone is brought in, having been caught trying to bury her brother; but apart from this it also sharpens our awareness of Créon's position, caught up in a situation of his own making, and stresses the legal and moral issues involved. The next few lines spoken by the chorus and Créon make it clear that this firmness of Créon's, and his intention of administering impartial justice ('Fust-il mon enfant propre') are laudable in themselves, and indeed necessary to the maintenance of a state:

CHOEUR DE VIEILLARDS:
> Vous voulez qu'un chacun ait son juste sallaire:
> Les uns de faire bien, les autres de malfaire.

CRÉON
> *Toute principauté en repos se maintient,*
> *Quand on rend à chacun ce qui luy appartient.*
> *Il faut le vicieux punir de son offense,*
> *Et que l'homme de bien le Prince recompense*
> *La peine et le loyer sont les deux fondemens,*
> Et les fermes piliers de tous gouvernemens.
>
> (Act IV, 1748–55)

Créon can, then, claim right on his side. Yet he seems to be in the wrong according to the final verdict of the chorus (see above, p. 48) and wrong on three counts. Firstly, the edict itself is iniquitous. Secondly, it is by no means clear that 'justice egale' ought to be extended to those of royal blood; the chorus says:

> Créon a vrayment tort
> De livrer à la mort
> Cette vierge *royale*.
> (Act IV, 2146–8)

(Similarly, there is the insistence in *Les Juifves* that Sédécie ought to be treated with the respect due to royalty.) Thirdly, Créon acts as a tyrant in disregarding public opinion:

HÉMON: Ce ne sera l'advis de la cité Thebaine.
CRÉON: Qu'ay-je affaire d'advis? Telle est ma volonté.
> (Act IV, 2033–4)

He goes still further when, although he has declared that he cannot relax the law that he has made, he declines to accept that he is bound by the established law:

HÉMON: N'estes-vous pas suget aux loix de la cité?
CRÉON: Un Prince n'est sujet aux loix de sa province.
HÉMON: Vous parlez d'un tyran, et non pas d'un bon Prince.
> (Act IV, 2035–7)

Hémon adds that 'la loy publique un Roy ne doit enfreindre'. By what compulsion is the king obliged to observe 'la loy publique'? From this passage it seems that it is in order to keep the love and respect of his subjects; this is implied by the use of 'aussi' in Hémon's speech:

> *Ils* [les sujets] *doivent au contraire obeir à leurs Rois,*
> *A leurs Rois leurs seigneurs, les aimer et les craindre:*
> Aussi la loy publique un Roy ne doit enfreindre.
> (Act IV, 2039–41)

Apparently there is no constitutional obligation, only a practical one; if the king does not show respect for the established law, he will lose the good will of his people; it is therefore worth his while to be law-abiding.

The other main aspect of the king's relationship with the law is the administration of justice, which involves not making, but determining law, and seeing to its application. There are many passages in Garnier indicating that adjudication is one of the king's functions. In *La Troade* Polymestor demands of Agamemnon:

> Revengez mon injure, ains la vostre: pourquoy
> Si ne faites justice estes vous esleu Roy?
>
> (Act v, 2609–10)

Not only is it the king's duty to administer justice but, according to Polymestor, he is appointed king for this end. Does 'esleu' suggest an idea of elective monarchy or merely refer to the fact that Agamemnon, though *hereditary* ruler of Mycenae, or Argos, was *elected* commander-in-chief over the other Greek princes for the Trojan expedition? The second interpretation seems impossible, since 'faire justice' was certainly not the purpose for which Agamemnon was placed in command of the Greek forces. It is interesting to compare this with a paragraph heading in Jean de la Madeleyne's *De l'estat et office d'un bon roy* (1575, four years before publication of *La Troade*): 'Les Roys esleus pour leur vertu et prudence'. La Madeleyne has a religious conception of the source of royal authority, but here he does not mean 'divinely appointed' but literally 'elected', for the example he gives is Henri III's election to the throne of Poland in 1574. Agamemnon does not dispute Polymestor's view of his function and proceeds to adjudicate, though his judgment is not in Polymestor's favour. Garnier seems very close here to the feeling expressed by Michel de l'Hospital in his speech before the King (François II) and Queen Mother at the Estates of Orléans, January, 1561. Speaking of how seemly it is for the king to summon the Estates and listen to their grievances, the Chancellor says: 'Les Roys ont esté esleuz premierement pour faire la justice, et n'est acte tant Royalle faire la guerre que faire justice.'[1] A little later he comments that: 'la bonne femme qui demandoit au Roy Philippes qui s'excusoit a elle disant qu'il n'avoit loisir de l'oyr, eust grande raison de luy reppliquer, Ne

---

[1] *La Harangue faicte par Monsieur le Chancelier de France le treziesme jour de janvier. Mil cinq centz soixante, estans les estatz convoques en la Ville d'Orleans, (s.l.n.d.),* A iii *verso.*

sois doncq Roy.'[1] In rather simpler syntax, Garnier's Polymestor is saying virtually the same thing.

The idea of the king as judge is also implicit in *Bradamante*
where Charlemagne states sententiously that a king should ask
for advice and not be hasty in his judgments:

> Je ne veux rien resoudre en affaire si grande,
> Que des gens de conseil advis je ne demande.
> *Un Roy qui tout balance au poix de l'equité,*
> *Doit juger toute chose avecque meureté.*
>
> (Act iv, 1397–1400)

And Hémon in *Antigone* had praised the king who is willing to
take advice:

> Ne ressemblez à ceux qui, pensant tout sçavoir,
> Ne veulent le conseil d'un autre recevoir.
> *Ce n'est point deshonneur à un Prince bien sage*
> *D'apprendre quelquefois d'un moindre personnage,*
> *Et suivre son advis, s'il le conseille bien,*
> *Sans par trop obstiner et arrester au sien.*
>
> (Act iv, 2014–19)

Thus Garnier attributes to the king both legislative and adjudi-
catory authority. This is not true of all sixteenth-century writers,
but the combination is found in many of the legists who, like
Garnier, had studied Roman law at Toulouse. 'The union, drawn
from Roman law, of *legislation* and *adjudication* in rulership was
important in the evolution of kingship from the medieval idea of
the monarch as *judge* to the later conception of a *law-making*
sovereign.'[2] But opinions vary: in contrast to the Roman legists
there is Estienne Pasquier, who denies that a king has the right
to make law. There were also several attempts to prove that the
Estates General were a legislative body. They were within a
hair's breadth of becoming one at the session of 1576–7, but the
project failed because of opposition from the Tiers Etat, led by
Jean Bodin. Bodin, (*Les VI Livres de la republique*, 1576) makes

---

[1] *Ibid.*, A iv *recto*.

[2] William Farr Church, *Constitutional thought in sixteenth-century France. A study
in the evolution of ideas* (Cambridge, Mass., 1941), p. 51.

legislative power the only true mark of sovereignty (in this he is followed by Le Roy) and says that the king cannot delegate this power without forfeiting sovereignty; but he points out that the opinion of the ancients was that kings were appointed chiefly to do justice; this point of view is held by many French writers, including one (Heluïs de Thillard) who considers that it is particularly true of the King of France. The opinion is in fact almost unanimous, in sixteenth-century France, that one of a king's primary functions, if not the most important of all, is to do justice. We find it expressed by writers of all varieties of political and religious allegiance, from the Protestant author of the *Reveille-matin* ('un prince qui refuse justice à un sien sujet est coupable devant Dieu') to the Catholics Jean Heluïs de Thillard and Jean de la Madeleyne, who both consider that a king is appointed by God for that purpose.

Thus in saying that it is the king's duty to do justice, Garnier is voicing a generally held opinion. On the question of a king's obedience to established law, opinions differ more widely. For one thing, some kinds of law may be more binding than others. Thus although some say that the king is bound by 'law', others specify that it is the 'lois fondamentales' or constitutional laws which are binding on a king—logically enough since they determined his own accession to the throne. In the Protestant camp, De Bèze (in *Du Droit des magistrats*, 1574) says that the prince is bound by the laws of his country because he has sworn to maintain them; Gousté, another Protestant, also considers that the Prince is formally required to observe existing laws (*Traicté de la puissance et authorité des roys*, 1561) and Jean de la Taille, probably a Protestant, affirms that the king must support the constitutional laws (in *Le Prince nécessaire*, his verse adaptation of Machiavelli's *Prince*). The 'politique' Estienne Pasquier, who believes that the king cannot make laws, also believes that he cannot break them (*Recherches de la France*, 1660). Sorbin, the Catholic royalist (confessor to Charles IX and editor of his *Tombeau*) says in his *Vray Reveille-matin* (1576) that the king has to submit himself voluntarily to laws, for none can force him to observe them. This is one of the trickiest problems raised by absolutist theories arising from the Roman law concept of 'princeps legibus solutus'; for even absolutists would like the king to act in accordance with law, but have to insist that he is not bound to do so; for what power can bind the 'loy vivante'? The reason why he should observe the law, according to Sorbin, is to set a good example to his subjects. This had also occurred to Guillaume Budé (*Institution du Prince*, Paris, 1547), who said that the king need not submit to law, but might choose to do so for the sake of example. Still thinking of the prince as a moral exemplar, Heluïs and La Madeleyne maintain that a prince should be even more law-abiding than his subjects, but unlike the Protestants they do not suggest by what authority he could be made to be so. Garnier's attitude here, as suggested by Hémon's speech to Créon in *Antigone* (quoted above, p. 67), seems to cut through the abstract debate with a strong note of pragmatic common sense. The king ought to observe law because otherwise he will lose the affection and respect of his subjects, which means personal danger for him. Here is no constitutional obligation or moral exhortation but a strong practical inducement.

The special aspect of the problem which concerns the degree of a king's obligation to his own edicts (as opposed to laws already in existence when he came to the throne) is also regarded variously. The view of Charlemagne's subjects is that a prince cannot break his own edict (modified by Aymon who says this is only true of an edict dealing with a weighty, public matter); Créon abides rigidly by his edict forbidding the burial of Polynice. These attitudes would be approved by Machiavelli, who says: 'I do not think there is any worse example in a state than to make a law and not observe it, especially if you made it yourself' (*Discorsi*, i, xlv);[1] and he speaks of the violation of law by the ruler both as a bad example, and a provocative offence which will rebound on to the ruler—in this he anticipates both the arguments used by sixteenth-century writers, with regard to law in general. But not all theorists take this line, and Bodin (with whose views Garnier's coincide at some other points) considers that a king can revoke his own laws, and that the legal phrase describing edicts as eternal and irrevocable is merely a

[1] My translation.

71

piece of bluff designed to make the edict seem impressive and sacrosanct to the populace. With this in mind, one might regard Créon's ritual restatement of his edict, and declaration that he cannot go back on it, as a similar piece of bluff or a warning to the Thebans of the importance he attaches to the decree.

Apart from the *clémence/rigueur* debate, which I shall discuss separately (in chapter 6), most of the other aspects of kingship mentioned by Garnier can be accounted for by the rhetorical requirements of the plays rather than by any connection with contemporary preoccupations. Thus the theme of the lure and burden of kingship is one that occurs both in Garnier's plays and in political writings (*Marc-Antoine*, *Cornélie*, *La Troade*, *Antigone*, *Les Juifves*; Symphorien Champier, Jean Heluïs, Pibrac, La Taille), but it is also extremely frequent in Seneca and I consider that Garnier's use of it is rhetorical rather than political. Indeed, in the political writers themselves it usually provides a rhetorical flourish. The same applies to the theme of the fall of a great monarch; this is very common in both Garnier and Seneca, and Garnier shows the consequent bitterness to be as intense for a tyrant as for a good king.[1] But the nearest that the political writers come to this theme is a warning that kings are more exposed to the blows of Fortune than are lesser men.

There is, however, one last aspect of Garnier's picture of kingship which is by definition non-Senecan, and that is the Christian conception of the king's dependence on God. Protestant writers tend to claim some degree of popular participation in the origin of kingship and the establishment of kings (e.g. 'Dieu eslit le roy et le peuple l'etablit'),[2] and they point to the Old Testament example of Saul, who became the first king of Israel because the people asked for a king. Catholic writers use the same illustration to emphasize that kings are chosen and established by God. In connection with this theme, there seems to be some evolution towards a specifically Catholic position in Garnier's thought; for the idea of the divine origin of kingship is stated explicitly in his last two plays. It may be objected that

---

[1] Garnier's treatment of the Tyrant is partly rhetorical and partly political; the subject will be discussed in chapter 7, with particular reference to Nabuchodonosor.

[2] Claude Gousté, *Traicté de la puissance et authorité des roys* (1561).

these are the only two plays where it could appear, as one is a religious tragedy, the other contains a Christian king, Charlemagne. But Garnier could have embodied it in the 'pagan' plays and indeed comes near to doing so in the third from last play, *Antigone*, where Antigone declares that laws are only valid if they are based on divine law:

> Le grand Dieu, qui le Ciel et la Terre a formé,
> Des hommes a les loix aux siennes conformé,
> Qu'il nous enjoint garder comme loix salutaires,
> Et celles rejetter qui leur seront contraires.
> Nulles loix de Tyrans ne doivent avoir lieu,
> Que lon voit repugner aux preceptes de Dieu.
>
> (Act iv, 1810–15)

This is Christian in feeling and tone; presumably Garnier did not feel that it clashed with its 'pagan' setting, any more than he felt a clash between the predominantly Roman and Christian associations of the subtitle of *Antigone* (Roman *pietas*, Christian piety and pity) and its Greek subject.[1] Thus he could have presented this religious point of view in other plays, and certainly he could have presented it in the *Hymne de la monarchie*. As he did not, we may suppose it to be an idea which developed during the period of his literary activity, so that by the time of writing *Bradamante* and *Les Juifves* he is in accord with Gallican constitutionalists like La Madeleyne or the very moderate Protestant author of the dialogue *Le Politique* in the *Memoires de l'estat de France sous Charles IX*. He is even close to the absolutists. Charlemagne's phrase:

> Les sceptres des grands Rois viennent du Dieu supréme,
>
> (*Bradamante*, Act i, 1)

is reminiscent of Le Roy's in the outline of his *Monarchiques* (1570): 'Les grandes monarchies sont divinement constituées.' In *Les Juifves* Sédécie points out that even a bad king is the

---

[1] 'Mixed theology' is very common in sixteenth-century literature; cf. the Witch of Endor in Jean de la Taille's *Saül*; not only is she called 'la Pythonisse' but the powers she invokes in her spellmaking include those of Hebrew and Greek mythology (e.g. the angels who fell with Lucifer from Olympus) and of French folklore.

image of God, so that in the person of Nabuchodonosor he is bound to respect:

> Le temple, la vertu, la semblance de Dieu.
>
> (Act IV, 1466)

This recalls both the description of Henri III, in the course of a highly critical speech by the *premier président* of the Paris Parlement in 1586, as 'l'ymage vivante de Dieu', and Claude d'Albon's insistence that good and bad princes alike are established by God and are images of the supreme ruler.[1]

In the *Hymne* if not in the plays, Garnier could also have indicated some awareness of two other topics much discussed by sixteenth-century political writers on kingship: the relationship between the Crown and the Church, and the king's claims on his subjects' property, his right to levy taxes, and his handling of finance in general. Apparently he found these rather technical subjects less interesting, or less important, than the more general questions concerning law and morals.

We may sum up Garnier's views on kings and kingship as they appear in his writings, as follows: the king is both judge and law-giver; it is his duty to do justice, to protect his people and their honour, and to set them a moral example. He expects obedience from his subjects, but cannot rightfully demand that they obey an immoral edict. It is doubtful whether he is free to ignore or revoke his own edicts. Although the idea of impartiality and 'justice égale' is meritorious, royal status requires privileged treatment (Sédécie, Antigone). The king ought to observe both 'la loy publique' and the force of public opinion. Finally, in Garnier's later plays we find the view that monarchical power originates with God and is dependent on him and that a king, even a bad one, is in some sense the image and vessel of God.

I have indicated in the course of this chapter some resemblances between Garnier and other political writers; but it would be premature to 'place' him politically before examining

---

[1] In *Harangue faite par le roy estant en son conseil le 16 juin* . . . (Paris, 1586) p. 15; Claude d'Albon, *De la majesté royalle* (1575) p. 5.

what he has to say on other political themes (war, tyrannicide, rebellion) and how his treatment of certain stock debates and historical figures (the *clémence/rigueur* debate, the figure of Nebuchadnezzar) compares with the use made of these subjects by other writers.

5

FOREIGN WAR AND CIVIL WAR

I devoted a whole chapter to the subject of monarchy and king-ship because this reflected the preponderant importance given to the topic by Garnier, which in turn coincided with the pre-occupations of contemporary theorists, whether they were primarily political philosophers or jurists. But Garnier's con-temporaries (not only the political theorists but every French-man) must have been painfully aware of one other political topic: war. War in general (with the constant danger of hostilities with Spain, England or the German states) and civil war in particular. This universal concern is certainly reflected in Garnier's plays; indeed, war forms the setting for many of them —either the Roman civil wars (*Cornélie, Porcie, Marc-Antoine*), the Trojan war (*La Troade*) or the war of the Seven against Thebes (*Antigone*). Of the other three plays, *Les Juifves* shows the aftermath of rebellion and the relationship of a tyrant to his defeated enemy; *Bradamante* starts just after the Moors have been defeated, with Charlemagne discussing what has to be done to repair the damage of war; and even *Hippolyte*, in which the subject has nothing to do with war, contains (Act I, p. 247) one image drawn from war, and an extremely odd image at that, as I hope to show later in this chapter.

Although civil war is, not surprisingly, the kind most often mentioned by Garnier, he also writes in several places of foreign war. Usually he mentions it in order to say that it is in some way preferable to civil war. Thus Jocaste urges Polynice to seek a kingdom not by attacking his native city but by undertaking a war of conquest in Lydia or elsewhere:

> Là vaudra beaucoup mieux vos forces employer
> Pour un sceptre nouveau que de nous guerroyer:

76

Vous y pourrez, sans crime, acquerre un diadême.
> (*Antigone*, Act II, 884–6)

The soldiers who form one of the three choruses in *Porcie* also compare foreign war favourably to civil, and they give their reason which is not a very noble one:

> C'est aux estranges régions,
> Qu'il fait bon pour les légions;
> C'est dedans ces terres barbares
> Que, faisant guerre, nous pouvions
> Soûler nos courages avares.
> (*Porcie*, Act III, p. 65)

When it comes to civil war, Garnier has rather more to say. In the final chorus of Act IV of *Cornélie*, for example, the supporters of Jule César pray that César and Rome may be protected from war and especially from 'civile fureur' (p. 149). Another chorus in *Porcie* asks why, if the gods wish to punish the arrogance of mighty Rome, they must choose as the means:

> Un si misérable discord
> En nos entrailles.
> (*Porcie*, Act IV, p. 80)

In *Cornélie*, Jule César expresses a disgust with civil war which is the more impressive for coming from a great and hardened warrior, who presumably has few scruples about war in general, but balks at fighting his fellow-citizens:

> J'atteste Jupiter qui tonne sur la terre,
> Que contraint malgré moy j'ay mené ceste guerre
> Et que victoire aucune, où j'apperçoy gésir
> Le corps d'un citoyen, ne me donne plaisir:
> Mais de mes ennemis l'envie opiniâtre
> Et le malheur romain m'a contraint de combatre.
> (*Cornélie*, Act IV, p. 144)

It is noticeable that César does not say that civil war is immoral, but rather that he finds it distasteful and emotionally painful, just as in *Porcie* the soldiers say:

Il me *desplaist* que les Romains
S'entre-massacrent de leurs mains,
Et que nos guerrières phalanges
Ne vont en quelques lieux lointains
Combatre les peuples estranges.

(Act III, p. 67 [my italics])

But the question of the morality of war, and of what constitutes a *iustum bellum*, does arise elsewhere. I have already pointed out that it arises by implication in Jocaste's exhortation to Polynice; but she does not go so far as to suggest that a war of aggression for conquest would be intrinsically good, only that it would be 'beaucoup mieux' than to continue his present wicked enterprise, and that he could undertake it 'sans crime'. In *Cornélie* Décie Brute implies that war for conquest is acceptable, both by his surprise when Cassie seem to suggest that:

La guerre seroit donc des hommes rejettable

(*Cornélie*, Act IV, p. 138)

and by his next reply to Cassie: Cassie says that war is detestable unless it is 'raisonnable' and Décie's answer, in defence of César, is:

Il a l'empire accreu de mainte nation.

This implies that war is legitimate if it increases the greatness of one's own country. Cassie does not explicitly reject this argument, but objects that César has been using war immorally, attacking the Gauls, 'un peuple innocent', without provocation in order to give his soldiers training before leading them on Rome:

On le devoit livrer pour expier la ville,
D'avoir sans cause esmeu l'Alemagne tranquille.
Il alloit irritant ces nations exprés
Pour nourrir une armée, et s'en aider aprés,
Contre le nom latin, l'attraînant aguerrie
Dans Rome pour ravir sa belle seigneurie.
[. . .]
Les Gaules à César estoyent un avant-jeu
Du discord citoyen qu'il a depuis esmeu.

(*Cornélie*, Act IV, p. 138)

César's war on the Gauls was immoral for two reasons: it was unprovoked, and it was undertaken with the immoral purpose of preparing his troops for civil war.

There remains one kind of war which can be approved of—that is, one side's part in it can be praiseworthy. To fight in defence of one's country is just and honourable, and to die in such a war is a fine death:

> Et quel plus grand honneur sçauroit-on acquerir
> Que sa douce patrie au besoin secourir?
> Se hazarder pour elle, et courageux respandre
> Tout ce qu'on a de sang, pour sa cause defendre?
> *Toute guerre est cruelle, et personne ne doit*
> *L'entreprendre jamais, sinon avecques droit:*
> *Mais si pour sa defense et juste et necessaire*
> *Par les armes il faut repousser l'adversaire,*
> *C'est l'honneur de mourir la pique dans le poing*
> *Pour sa ville, et l'avoir de sa vertu tesmoing.*
> (*La Troade*, Act I, 403–12, Cassandre to Hécube)

The same notion of the glory of a patriotic death (which is of course a classical commonplace) is expressed by the chorus of soldiers in *Porcie*:

> Il n'est trespas plus glorieux
> Que de mourir audacieux
> Parmi les troupes combatantes,
> Que de mourir devant les yeux
> De tant de personnes vaillantes.
>
> O trois et quatre fois heureux,
> Ceux qui d'un fer avantureux
> Se voyent arracher la vie,
> Avecques un coeur généreux
> Se consacrans à la patrie.
> (*Porcie*, Act III, p. 66)

But earlier in the same play the value of a glorious patriotic death had been disputed by Porcie, who points out how futile it can be:

NOURRICE: Qui meurt pour le païs vit éternellement.
PORCIE: Qui meurt pour des ingrats meurt inutilement.
> (*Porcie*, Act II, p. 38)

Thus any praise of legitimate war, and of a patriotic death in defence of one's home, is modified by the expression of disapproval of war in general ('Toute guerre est cruelle') and by the ironical casting of doubt on such a well-worn commonplace as Horace's *dulce et decorum est, pro patria mori*.

In addition to mentioning various kinds of war and showing different attitudes to it, Garnier also discusses several aspects of the aftermath of war. In *La Troade*, Hécube and Cassandre draw up a kind of balance sheet of suffering, showing that the two sides have perhaps suffered equally:

> Les miseres des Grecs sont aux nostres egales.
>
> (Act I, 358)

Although the Trojans have lost the war, their men at least had the comfort of fighting a just war, on their own soil, watched and encouraged by their womenfolk, while the Greeks fought far from home, and lost as many great heroes as the Trojans. Moreover, for some Greeks the worst is yet to come: a difficult journey, or a home-coming to treachery and death. The same theme of the high cost of victory, with both sides finding themselves sick and diminished at the end of the war, is expressed by a chorus in *Antigone*:

> Ils ont receu pareil esclandre:
> [. . .]
> Ils ne sont pas plus demeurez
> De nos soldats en ces guerez,
> Que de leur outrageuse armee.
> S'ils pensent nous avoir vaincus,
> C'est d'une victoire Cadmee,
> Où les vainqueurs pleurent le plus.
>> (*Antigone*, Act III, 1496–1505)

Garnier shows some attitudes of both the defeated and the victor at the end of a war. In *La Troade* we see two reactions on the defeated side. In Andromaque, fear:

HELEN: Des vainqueurs ennemis le colere ne dure.
ANDROMAQUE: Il me sera tousjours en pareille terreur.
HELEN: Il ne faut qu'eviter la premiere fureur.

> (*La Troade*, Act II, 710–12)

In Hécube, helpless fury and the desire for revenge:

> Or vous, Grecs frauduleux, qui d'armes deloyales
> Avez renversé Troye aux ondes Stygiales:
> [. . .]
> Qui par vos cruautez avez pollu la terre,
> L'onde humide et le ciel, [. . .]
> Puisse, pour nous venger de vos lasches parjures,
> Neptun vous travailler d'horribles avantures
> [. . .]
> Bref, que, si tost qu'aurez esloigné ceste rade,
> Vous souffriez comme nous des maux une Iliade.
> (*La Troade*, Act IV, 2179–80, 2183–4, 2187–8, 2211–12)

This speech sums up all the pathos and savagery in the figure of Hécube: the pathos of the bereaved mother, wife and queen, and the savagery which drives her to take horrible revenge on the only one of her enemies to fall within her diminished power—Polymestor.

Garnier deals more fully and more interestingly with the other side, the victors. Both morally and practically, the victor has more and harder decisions to make, and these Garnier examines in some detail. One such dilemma of victory occurs in Garnier's earliest play, *Porcie*, where Marc-Antoine and Octave discuss how to treat the remnant of the defeated conspirators and their supporters. Marc-Antoine thinks it is sufficient to have defeated, despoiled and banished them, but Octave insists that:

> Ce n'est encore assez, ils devroyent estre morts.
> (*Porcie*, Act III, p. 59)

His reason seems to be partly a feeling that the murderers of Caesar, and those murderers' allies, should receive the severest possible punishment, and only death meets this requirement; and partly the practical consideration that victory is not assured unless the enemy is completely destroyed, because:

> On sçait combien Fortune a les pieds incertains.
> (*Ibid.*, p. 60)

It is interesting to see that it is the braggart soldier Marc-Antoine who shrinks from the idea of more slaughter (just as we noticed earlier that the successful general Jule César spoke with loathing of civil war).[1] The implication is that Marc-Antoine, a type of the great soldier, is ready to stop fighting when his own honour is satisfied, and has neither political calculation nor tyrannical blood-lust to impel him to a thorough extermination of his enemies. In *Cornélie*, on the other hand, Marc-Antoine is cast as the canny, realistic adviser to the generous victor (Jule César) who supposes that his enemies will be grateful to him for magnanimously sparing their lives:

CÉSAR: Ceux conspirer ma mort qui la vie ont de moy?
MARC-ANTOINE: Aux ennemis domtez il n'y a point de foy.
CÉSAR: En ceux qui vie et biens de ma bonté reçoivent?
MARC-ANTOINE: Voire, mais beaucoup plus à la patrie ils doivent.
(Cornélie, Act IV, pp. 145–6)

Octave's combination of the desire for retribution or revenge and the need to make sure that victory is complete is seen again in Charlemagne, but with much more emphasis on the second element. The debate between him and Nymes (*Bradamante*, Act I) is totally unimportant from the point of view of the play's action; it is as though Garnier cannot keep away from the subject:

CHARLEMAGNE: Nous contenterons-nous de les vaincre à demy?
NYMES: Ne vous suffit-il pas de chasser l'ennemy?
CHARLEMAGNE: Ce ne m'est pas assez de defendre ma terre.
NYMES: Que demandez-vous plus que d'achever la guerre?
CHARLEMAGNE: Un Empereur Romain ne se peut dire avoir
  Pour chasser un Barbare assez fait de devoir,
  Qui pourra retourner avec nouvelle force.
(Bradamante, Act I, 123–9)

As this discussion develops, the emperor's argument relies exclusively on the practical dangers, so that the suggestion of another motive (such as the *gloire* of a Holy Roman Emperor) is comparatively slight and unimportant. A Christian king, in other words, pursues his defeated enemy only in order to make sure that the enemy cannot launch a new attack. As a humane commander, Agamemnon (in *La Troade*) also thinks along

---

[1] Jule César's speech in *Cornélie*, Act IV (see p. 77, above).

these lines: Troy has been convincingly defeated and there is
no need for more slaughter among the ruins. Even the sack of
Troy went further than he wished:

> Aussi le ciel j'atteste, et le throsne des Dieux
> Qu'onques je n'eus vouloir d'abatre, furieux,
> Les Pergames de Troye, et de mettre à l'espee
> Par un sac inhumain cette terre occupee.
> Sans plus je desirois voir leur coeur endurci
> Contraint à demander de leur faute merci:
> Mais du soldat ne peut l'outrageuse insolence
> Tellement se domter qu'il n'use de licence,
> Quand la nuict, la victoire, et le courroux luy ont
> Acharné le courage, et mis l'audace au front.
>   Donc ce qui est resté de sa rage, demeure;
> C'est assez, je ne veux qu'aucun de sang froid meure.
> (La Troade, Act III, 1419–30)

His moderation is dictated not only by humanity, but by the
awareness that:

> Nous sommes au lieu mesme où elle [Troye] souloit estre.
> La fortune, Priam, qui te rend si chetif,
> Certes me fait ensemble et superbe et craintif.
> (Ibid., 1410–12)

His attitude here is contrasted with that of Pyrrhe, who argues
that:

> *Ce qui plaist au vaincueur est loisible de faire.*
> (Ibid., 1485)

It is rare for a conqueror to feel Agamemnon's humility and
caution, to be so well aware that his luck could change; more
often it is an adviser or confidant, or a defeated enemy, who puts
this point of view to an over-complacent victor; examples of this
are Hécube's warning to Pyrrhe (*La Troade*, Act III, 1581–4),
and the Queen's to Nabuchodonosor (*Les Juifves*, Act III, 937–
42). The theme of capricious Fortune, even less reliable in war
than in other fields of action, was one for which contemporary
events provided ample illustration, in the shifting vicissitudes of
the religious wars—the brilliant victories which proved worth-
less, the painstakingly drafted treaties which were dishonoured

a few weeks later, the wearisome sieges more costly to the winner than the loser. Of no war was it more true to remark:

> Combien Mars est instable, et que le sort humain
> Est tousjours, mais sur tout aux combats, incertain.
>
> (*Antigone*, Act iii, 892–3)[1]

But if the conqueror has to decide how far to pursue his victory, and remind himself of the precarious nature of his own success, there are also positive and constructive tasks awaiting his attention. These are mentioned by Charlemagne, who at the beginning of *Bradamante* leaves unsettled the question of whether to carry the war beyond the frontiers of France, and talks of the things to be done at home:

> Il nous faut rebastir nos Eglises rompues,
> Oû se sont par sur tout leurs cruautez repues:
> Rebastir nos citez de murailles et tours,
> Repeupler de paisans nos villages et bourgs.
>
> (*Bradamante*, Act i, 153–6)

And in addition to reorganization and physical repairs he must 'rappeler les vertus exilees', driven out by war, and recompense those who shared in the victory.

This programme of reconstruction, set out so briskly and confidently, strikes one as the positive side of Garnier's vision of war; if he has such clear notions of the reconstruction needed after a war, it is because he is willing to see, and able to describe, the destruction and suffering that any war produces. He does not shy away from horror, grief and desolation, but insists that we share his imaginative visions of these things, whether it is the bleak, abandoned countryside round Thebes (*Antigone*) or the humiliation of prisoners of war in Troy or Antioch (*La Troade, Les Juifves*). Sometimes it seems as though a subject of this kind has seized on his imagination so strongly that it receives a treatment out of proportion to its relevance or importance in the context. This is the case with the image in *Hippolyte* which I mentioned earlier. In later editions, Garnier suppressed four lines of this image, but this is how it appears in the 1573

---

[1] Cf. *Porcie*, Act iii, pp. 60–61; *Marc-Antoine*, Act iii, p. 208.

edition, at the point in Egée's monologue where he describes the subjection of Athens to Crete, and the annual tribute of young men and women for the Minotaur:

> Tandis que j'ay vescu, je t'ay veu, ma Cité,
> Tousjours porter au col une captivité,
> Non telle que l'on voit en une ville prise,
> Qu'un roy victorieux humainement maistrise,
> Subjuguée à ses loix, sans luy estre cruel,
> Et luy rien exiger qu'un tribut annuel,
> Qu'entre mille citez la chétive veincue,
> Gémissant et platrant, malgré soy contribue.
> Mais en ta servitude, ô Athènes, le sort
> Menaçoit tes enfans d'une cruelle mort.
> (*Hippolyte*, Act I, pp. 247–8, p. 338)

Obviously something very odd has happened here. Egée is supposed to be comparing the relatively painless lot of a normal conquered city, governed 'humainement' and 'sans luy estre cruel' by a victorious king, with that of Athens which by 'une ordonnance inique' has to send fourteen human victims for the Minotaur every year. But somehow the idea gets out of hand, and the two lines 'Qu'entre mille . . . malgré soy contribue' contain such strong emotional colouring that the conquered city itself stirs the reader's pity, instead of merely providing a foil for the pitiable state of Athens. Garnier cut out the inconsistency in later editions by breaking off the description after 'maistrise'; but the fact that he wrote it at all is an example of his insistence on the miseries of war, the humiliation, poverty and suffering which the conquered must endure even, he suggests here, under a humane conqueror. This passage is not a typical one to illustrate Garnier's writing on war; it is incidental to the main theme of the play in which it occurs, and indeed is irrelevant and illogical in its context. There are many passages which show Garnier's concern more directly, and I shall quote only a few of the more striking examples. Any of the plays would provide them, but I shall quote from *Porcie*, *Cornélie* and *Antigone*. In the two earlier plays, Garnier reaches the horror and grotesqueness of nightmare in his descriptions of battlefields: here is no heroic grandeur, no glorification of the soldier's death, but noise, mess,

mutilation and pain, brought more urgently before the reader by
the use of 'vous', while in *Cornélie* the horror is increased by the
'homely' images of the sponge and the wine-press.

> Là vous n'eussiez ouy qu'un craquètement d'armes,
> Là vous n'eussiez rien veu qu'un meurtre de gensdarmes,
> Qui durement navrez trébuschoyent plus espois
> Que ne sont en hyver les fueillages aux bois.
> L'un a les bras tronquez, ou la cuisse avalée,
> L'autre une autre partie en son corps mutilée;
> Vous n'oyez que souspirs des blessez qui mouroyent,
> Que menaces et cris de ceux qui demeuroyent:
> Vous n'aviez sous les pieds que chevaus et gensdarmes,
> Que picques et pavois, que divers outils d'armes,
> Qui gisoyent sur le champ, demy noyez du sang,
> Qui flottoit par la plaine ainsi qu'en un estang.
>
> (*Porcie*, Act iv, pp. 71–2)

> On ne voyoit qu'horreur, que soldars encombrez
> Sous le faix des chevaus, que des corps démembrez
> Nageans dans leur sang propre, et des piles dressées
> D'hommes qui gémissoyent, sous les armes pressées,
> Coulant comme un esponge, ou l'amas raisineux
> Qu'un pesant fust escache en un pressouer vineux.
> Aux uns vous eussiez veu la teste my-partie
> Et la cervelle auprès qui tramblottoit sortie;
> Les uns percez à jour, les autres soustenoyent
> De leurs mourantes mains leurs boyaux qui traînoyent . . .
>
> (*Cornélie*, Act v, p. 159)

In *Antigone* there is particular emphasis on two other aspects of
suffering: the devastation of the countryside, and the fact that it
is 'le peuple' who bear the heaviest burden, rather than the
leaders whose quarrels have caused the war. A chorus lament in
Act ii combines these two themes:

> Cependant que le peuple en endure,
> C'est luy qui porte tout le faix.
> Car encor qu'il n'en puisse mais,
> Il leur sert tousjours de pasture.

> Mars dedans la campagne bruit,
> Nostre beau terroir est destruit:
> Le vigneron quitte la vigne,
> Le courbe laboureur ses boeus,
> Le berger ses pastis herbeus,
> Et le morne pescheur sa ligne.
> (*Antigone*, Act II, 974–83)

Without analysing at this point the particular qualities of such descriptions, and discussing what makes them more than rhetorical set-pieces, it is enough for the purposes of this chapter to notice their presence, in order to complete this survey of what Garnier says about war.

How do Garnier's statements and comments on war compare with Seneca's?

The first point that strikes one is that Seneca says little about war. This is not surprising as the conflicts in Seneca's plays are usually within a family (*Medea*, *Thyestes*, *Octavia*); this family conflict may enlarge to become a civil war (*Phoenissae*), but on the whole, Senecan strife, though great in intensity, is confined to a small group of people.

Let us examine briefly what Seneca does have to say about war. He deals with two themes. One is the proper conduct of the victor when war is over; but this is really, when most nobly expressed (by Agamemnon, arguing with Pyrrhus, in *Troades*), part of the kingship theme, and of the identification of the good king with the good man, or Stoic sage. This enlargement of the theme does not occur in Garnier. In Seneca it is brought about by the sententious, completely general nature and wording of some of the arguments used, e.g.:

> Quod non vetat lex, hoc vetat fieri pudor.
> (*Troades*, 334)

Such a principle could apply to a much wider field of moral problems than those faced by a victorious general. In *Hercules furens*, on the other hand, when Lycus argues with Hercules's wife on the value of peace to both sides, saying that peace is useful to the victor and necessary to the defeated (*Herc. fur.*, 368) and that:

87

cum victor arma posuit, et victum decet
deponere odia

(409–10)

the sententious nature of his words is given an ironical twist by the fact that he is not speaking frankly, but is trying to persuade Megara to marry him in order to strengthen his position on a usurped throne. This means that the audience does not listen to these lines as a 'straight' exposition of what must be done after the end of a war; since the speaker is not in good faith the words are not interesting or important for their straightforward virtue or application, but as part of a deceitful scheme by the villain of the play. In Garnier, on the contrary, the theme of peace being useful to the victor and necessary to the vanquished is voiced by a trustworthy character, Arée:

> Embrassez donc la paix, que lon dit en vulgaire
> Estre utile au vainqueur, au vaincu nécessaire.
> (*Porcie*, Act iii, p. 50)

The other 'war' topic mentioned several times by Seneca is civil war. His main theme is the wickedness of civil war: even the wicked Nero considers civil war an offence against moral law, as when he speaks of:

> impie gestum diu
> civile bellum.
> (*Octavia*, 523–4)

The same word is used by Antigone when she is trying to persuade Oedipus to return to Thebes and put an end to the fighting between his two sons Eteocles and Polynices:

> tu impii belli minas
> avertere unus [. . .] potes.
> (*Phoenissae*, 290–1)

And she links war and wrongdoing a few lines later when she begs Oedipus:

> prohibe pariter et bellum et scelus.
> (*Phoenissae*, 327)[1]

---

[1] In some editions the speech in which this line occurs is attributed to a *nuntius*.

Oedipus himself describes his sons, leaders of a civil war, as devoid of natural virtue, lacking love for father or fatherland, and drunk with ambition. Later in the play, Jocasta urges Polynices to seek another kingdom by arms—that is, a war of aggression and conquest against another country would be less evil than the war in his own country which he is carrying on at present (a piece of Machiavellian doctrine *avant la lettre*); and she points out not only the immorality, but also the folly of Polynices's action, which is destroying what he seeks to possess.

It should be pointed out that the war between Polynices and Eteocles is not purely a civil war, as Polynices has brought foreign allies with him to help him reduce Thebes. This increases his guilt, but is not the main part of it: what makes this war 'impium' and puts it on a level with 'scelus' is that he is fighting his own brother in their own country, an act both criminal and foolish.

We have seen that Seneca only deals with a restricted number of subjects connected with war; his *sententiæ* on the proper conduct of a victor express a general loftiness of aim and principle befitting the conduct of any virtuous man in many situations. As to war itself, Seneca, like Garnier, is mostly concerned with civil war, which he sees as an offence against God and against reason. He does not discuss what constitutes a just war, or whether such a thing exists (except to imply that an unprovoked war of conquest would be a meritorious undertaking for Polynices, or at least one that his parents could approve of, as compared to his attack on Thebes). Nor does Seneca discuss at any length the hardships and suffering caused by war.

Comparing this with Garnier we see considerable differences in content and emphasis between the two. What these differences add up to is a much greater stress, in Garnier, on the horror and misery of war and the sufferings and difficulties encountered by both sides. Seneca shows often enough in his theatre that he is attracted to the description of scenes of cruelty and horror, but his apparent aim is to give his listeners a macabre thrill rather than rouse their indignation or pity; therefore he chooses incidents of individual violence and brutality, not the wider pictures of devastated countryside and ruined towns.

Let us now briefly note how Garnier's themes and attitudes compare with those of more explicitly political writers, whether polemical or theoretical. There is less material to deal with here than in the case of kingship, as these questions on the nature and limitations of sovereignty attracted some of the finest legal minds of the age, who had much less to offer with regard to a less abstract subject such as war. But the subject, nevertheless, is dealt with by a spread of writers ranging from the Protestant Nicolas Barnaud (if the attribution to him of the *Miroir des Francois* (1581) is correct) to the courtier-priest and propagandist Arnault Sorbin, in his *Vray Reveille-matin* of 1576, a reply to the Calvinist *Reveille-matin*. War was also an important subject in the writings of Machiavelli, and some sixteenth-century French writers were influenced almost unconsciously by his thought.

I shall deal with various 'war-themes' in the same order as I discussed their occurrence in Garnier, but first, a point which I have already examined with reference to Garnier in chapter 3. This is the parallel between Roman and French history and particularly between the civil wars that marked the end of the Republic, and the French wars of religion. I pointed out (in chapter 3) Garnier's obvious interest in this parallel, but he is not the only writer to comment on it. The idea of such a parallel is implicit throughout Le Roy's *Exhortation aux Francois* (1570), and probably derives from his cyclical view of history, a view which also seems to be held by Garnier. In his *Consideration sur l'histoire françoise* (1567), Le Roy writes that the historian's task is to: 'advertir des vicissitudes de la fortune, pour n'admirer rien comme nouveau et estimer ne nous advenir chose qui ne soit advenue par le passé, et n'advienne cy apres.' (p. 13 *verso*.) He expressed the same view in *De la Vicissitude ou varieté des choses en l'univers*, published in 1579; Garnier's presentation of this philosophy can be seen in *Cornélie*, the final chorus of Act ii, p. 115. The parallel between Roman and French history is also pointed out by Jean de la Madeleyne, in chapter 20 of his treatise *De l'estat et office d'un bon roy, prince ou monarque* (1575), when he quotes Roman commentators who warned of the moral degeneration of the Roman republic and the disaster this would lead to, and remarks: 'Et pour dire vray, nous croyons que les remonstrances ne pourroyent estre tant propres et veritables en leur temps, comme elles pourroyent estre au nostre.' (p. 50 *verso*.) Jean Bodin, discussing the question of how to prevent civil war, says he will take the Roman wars as an example—and exclaims in a parenthesis 'pleust or à Dieu, que nous eussions faute d'exemples domestiques' (*République*, book v, chapter 5, p. 587). And it was a commonplace of sixteenth-century thought that one studied history in order to apply its lessons to similar situations in one's own time, which was why it was such an important subject in the education of a prince. Baïf wanted the young Henri III to spend part of his time 'discourant des histoires antiques' and in this he resembles any other of the many writers who composed an 'Institution du prince'.[1] Thus, the fact that Garnier seems aware of a parallel between another period of history and his own does not at all suggest that he is under the influence of any one political theorist or historiographer, but does tend to link him to a certain line of sixteenth-century didacticism.

In their analyses of Roman history, the French writers try to examine the causes of the Roman civil wars. Le Roy varies between an astrological explanation (*Consideration*, pp. 9 *verso*, 10 *recto*) which he later rejects as un-Christian, and the opinion that God sends such adversities as a check on a nation corrupted by too much prosperity (*Des Differens et troubles advenans entre les hommes*, 1563, p. 13 *recto*). La Madeleyne typifies those who present a moral explanation of factions, sedition and civil war, when he quotes Quintus Metellus Numidius on Rome: 'qu'on avoit deslogé et chassé hors de leur ville, la vertu et discipline ancienne, et que en son lieu on avoit receu toute ambition et avarice.' The predictable result was: 'la briefve ruine et revolution de leur Republicque, comme de faict elle avint bien tost apres

[1] J. A. de Baïf, *Epistre au Roy* (1575) p. 6 *verso*.

91

avec grands meurtres, fuites, et guerres civiles inhumaines, et plus que barbares, avec mutation de leur estat'. (*De l'Estat et office*, pp. 50 *recto*, 50 *verso*.)

Here he is close to Garnier who in *Cornélie* makes Cicéron list

> Méchante Ambition, des courages plus hauts
> Poison enraciné
>
> (Act I, p. 97)

as one of the main causes of the downfall of Rome, and elsewhere castigates avarice, luxury and *auri sacra fames*.

We can now come to the other topics discussed by Garnier, as set out in the earlier part of this chapter, and the first of these is the relationship between foreign and civil war. In Garnier this relationship is usually presented by a comparison between them, showing a preference for foreign war (Jocaste, the Roman legionaries in *Porcie*); in the political writers the angle is usually slightly different, though they are saying the same thing: the point they are making is that foreign war is useful because it averts civil war, by uniting the country against a foreign enemy (see chapter 3, pp. 36–7, for a discussion of the relevance of this principle in sixteenth-century France). The French writers usually point to Roman models to justify this strategy, but they could have found a more modern example in Machiavelli. In chapter XXI of the *Prince*, he praises Ferdinand of Aragon for employing it:

> At the start of his reign he attacked Granada; and this campaign laid the foundation of his power. First, he embarked on it undistracted, and without fear of interference; he used it to engage the energies of the barons of Castile who, as they were giving their minds to the war, had no mind for causing trouble at home.[1]

As in so many other problems Bodin (who is much closer to Machiavelli than he admits) has the same solution to offer, but he backs it with the authority of the Romans, of whom he says: 'le seul moyen qu'on trouvoit pour appaiser les seditions, estoit de faire guerre aux ennemis, et s'il n'y en avoit, d'en forger de

[1] *The Prince*, trans. George Bull (Harmondsworth, 1961) p. 120.

tous nouveaux.' (*Les VI Livres de la republique*, book iv, chapter 7, p. 496)

Later he expands this slightly:

mais je retourne aux exemples des anciens [. . .] pour monstrer qu'il est bien difficile, et presque impossible, de maintenir les sugets en paix, et amitié, s'ils ne sont en guerre contre l'ennemy. [. . .] Qui fut cause que le Senat entretenoit les guerres, et forgeoit des ennemis s'il n'y en avoit, pour se guarentir des guerres civiles.

(Ibid., book v, chapter 5, p. 587)

Le Roy confines himself to the example of France herself:

La France environ cent ans estoit demeuree en grande prosperité, jettant hors et au loing les guerres qu'il luy convenoit faire. Mais si tost qu'elle a cuidé se delivrer de l'ennemy estranger, elle en a trouvé de domestiques qui l'ont pirement traittee; ainsi que la paix exterieure cause ordinairement és estats publiques, dissention interieure.

(Exhortation aux Francois, p. 6 recto)

This attitude to war is not a partisan viewpoint (although obviously it would find support within different parties at different times, depending on whether the likeliest foreign enemy at the moment was Spain, England, or the German Protestant states) and we find it not only in the theoretical work of a Bodin, but in the propaganda writings of a Barnaud, who makes his character Scipion ('personnage bien entendu en l'art militaire') say: 'Je croy certainement qu'il n'y a moyen plus propre pour appaiser les François, que d'aller faire la guerre sur l'estranger.' He does add that the French ought not to settle their differences at the expense of 'un pauvre peuple qui n'a que faire de nos questions et debats', but his friend Milo ('un excellent commissaire des guerres') answers only the first part of Scipion's speech: 'C'est assavoir que le plus beau moyen de conserver un Estat, et le garantir de rebellions, seditions et guerres civiles, et d'entretenir les sujets en bonne amitié, est d'avoir un ennemy auquel on puisse faire teste.'[1]

---

[1] *Le Miroir des Francois, compris en trois livres* [. . .] *par Nicolas de Montand* (attrib. to Nicolas Barnaud) (*s.l.*, 1581) book ii, pp. 362–3.

This question of the function of foreign war in staving off civil war raises two others: is there such a thing as *iustum bellum* (for instance, can a foreign war be considered morally right, or legitimate, if it is undertaken to avert sedition at home?), and in what sense is civil war 'worse' than foreign war—more immoral, or simply more painful and more destructive?

To deal with the second of these questions first, most of the French political writers are curiously perfunctory when they consider the specific evils of civil war. La Taille is a typical example. In his *Prince nécessaire* he says that his prince should aim at 'paix civile' at any price, but does not explain why civil war is worse than other kinds:

> la paix civile [. . .]
> Qui, faicte a quelque pris qu'on vueille, est nécessaire;
> Mais la guerre civile est tousjours au contraire.

And again:

> Car on doit préférer la paix tousjours utile,
> Quelque bon droit qu'on ait, à la guerre civile.
> (*Œuvres*, iv, p. 100)

Perhaps, as the horror of civil war was all around them and their readers, most French writers felt it unnecessary to point out the ways in which it was bad. Two of the worst things about the French civil wars were that they involved so much emotional suffering in the divisions within communities and families, and that the fighting was never tidily restricted to one part of the country. Foreign war might have been more localized, and would certainly have been less emotionally harrowing. Some writers do go into this kind of detail, and one who does is Louis Le Roy. He uses the same expression as La Taille in speaking of peace: 'estant toute paix entre eux [i.e. les Français] plus utile que la guerre civile'; but he also gives reasons for this view, saying for example that civil war ('un si grand et horrible mal') causes suffering throughout the country, with loss of property and impoverishment; that it destroys normal love of country; that it divides provinces, cities and families, setting 'peres contre fils,

freres contre freres, oncles contre nepveux'; and that, as Cicero
pointed out to the Romans, civil wars cannot be concluded without 'l'occision des principaux de la Cité, avec la diminution du
peuple et calamité de la Republique'.[1]

The particular form of civil war in which Polynices engaged
(when he used foreign allies to help him destroy the kingdom
which he hoped to win) is also singled out for comment by Le
Roy, in the same work; the first occasion is when he describes
the leaders of civil strife as 'tant irresolus le plus souvent, qu'ils
ayment plustost se submettre indignement à l'estranger, sous
esperance de se fortifier de luy, que par honnestes moyens se
reconcilier.' (*Exhortation aux Francois*, p. 11 *recto*.) Later he
praises the followers of the defeated Pompey, who were so
patriotic that they were loth to expose Caesar, their hated foe,
to the risk of defeat by the Parthians: 'Helas Seigneurs François
vous faittes bien autrement, gastans la France vostre patrie,
vostre mere, et nourrice: et appellans à parachever de la gaster,
estrangers de toutes parts, en intention d'assouvir voz courroux
et vengeances.' (*Ibid.*, p. 63 *verso*.)

Thus on questions concerning civil war we can find attitudes
similar to Garnier's among his contemporaries both Catholic
and Protestant. What about the definition of *iustum bellum*? On
the whole, sixteenth-century writers are cautious about this to
the point of evasiveness. After Seyssel (*La Grand' Monarchie*,
1519), no-one seems willing to give a definition. Sorbin an-
nounces in his table of contents that part of his book will examine
'de quelles parties doit estre composée une juste guerre' but he
hardly keeps his promise.[2] Most writers beg the question by
falling back on a quotation from Livy (IX, i) used by Machiavelli
in the *Prince* (chapter XXVI) and in the *Discorsi* (book III,
chapter XII); Claudius Pontius is supposed to have said to his
Samnite soldiers, when Rome forced them to fight by refusing
peace offers, 'Iustum est bellum quibus necessarium, et pia arma
ubi nulla nisi in armis spes est'.[3] When used in an appropriate

---

[1] *Exhortation aux Francois* (1570) pp. 2 *verso*, 3 *recto*, 5 *verso* and 10 *recto*.
[2] *Le Vray Resveille-matin des calvinistes et republicains françois* (Paris, 1576) p. 13
verso.
[3] This is the form in which Machiavelli gives the phrase; it is a misquotation,

context, as by Machiavelli and by Bodin (*Republique*, book v, chapter 5, p. 596) this is obviously not a definition of legitimate war at all, but an encouragement to fight hard when there is no alternative to fighting. But often the first half alone is quoted or translated, and offered as a definition of 'juste guerre' without, however, any criterion of 'necessity' being given. Pasquier in the *Pourparler du prince* (first published 1560) says that war should be undertaken only if necessary *and* just—but does not define either term. Bodin tells us that 'juste guerre' is one legitimate way for a prince to acquire a throne—but he does not tell us what constitutes such a war. I suspect that the vagueness of terminology reflects a vagueness of thought. One thing on which all were agreed was that war in self-defence, or rather, in defence of the *patria*, was legitimate, and even positively good. But after that, the picture becomes a little blurred, probably because to sixteenth-century French observers, a foreign war whether defensive or aggressive offered a tempting solution to the problem of how to stop the civil wars. Since the civil wars were destroying the country, an unprovoked attack on a foreign country could be construed as an action in defence of the *patria* (and therefore legitimate, even laudable) because it would unite the country against a common enemy. There is also a tendency to regard war as a princely art (*the* princely art, said Machiavelli), even while speaking of the king as primarily judge, lawgiver or father of his people. It is easy to see why no sixteenth-century French political writer examines the question rigorously. It will be remembered that there was also uncertainty in Garnier's position here. Like most of his contemporaries, he concedes that war in defence of the *patria* is legitimate and praiseworthy, and that a patriot's death is a noble one; but again, the picture is blurred, in this case by Garnier's revulsion from all war ('Toute guerre est cruelle') which leads him also to cast doubt on the value of a heroic death in battle.

We noticed that Garnier has a good deal to say about the

---

but the difference is in wording not in meaning. Livy's text in fact runs:
Iustum est bellum quibus necessarium et pia arma quibus nulla nisi in armis relinquitur spes.

aftermath of war—about the misery of both sides, and the proper conduct of victor and vanquished. In particular, he several times presents a debate as to how a conqueror (or the winning general in a civil war) should behave towards the remnant of his defeated enemies. Machiavelli had very decided views on this; his advice was that his prince should exterminate the ruling family of a conquered country (*Prince*, chapter III, chapter IV); the reason is that: 'When that has been wiped out there is no-one left to fear.'[1] Michel de l'Hospital considers that to leave alive the leaders of factions or conspiracies is dangerous; but as he is a man of peace and tolerance, his remedy is not to exterminate them at the end of the war, but to take this danger into account as an argument for stopping the war before it reaches its logical, bloody conclusion.[2]

This is surely a view with which Garnier would sympathize; we saw in *La Troade* how Agamemnon spoke of the difficulties of stopping hostilities, and in *Cornélie* how César shrank from the thought of having to carry his campaign to just the sort of extreme that L'Hospital envisages with alarm.

L'Hospital also anticipates Garnier when, in the same pamphlet, he speaks of the moral sickness that results from war, 'le mespriz et contemnement de l'authorité du roy, des loyx, et de la justice', a thought similar to that of Charlemagne in *Bradamante*, Act I, when he comments on how vice has flourished in his empire during the recent war.

I said earlier that the sixteenth-century theorists and pamphleteers are on the whole reticent about the nature of civil war; but this does not mean that they do not mention or describe the conditions which civil war is producing in France. What is missing is the juridical or philosophical analysis of whether civil war is essentially different from, or worse than, any other kind, and if so, why and how. But there are plenty of laments about the ruin of France; Le Roy's are the most abundant and they are

---

[1] This 'Machiavellian' principle (*Prince*, trans. G. Bull, chapter IV, p. 46) is already observed in the Trojan tragedies of Euripides and Seneca, by the Greeks who insist on killing Astyanax, the only male survivor of the Trojan royal family.

[2] *Discours sur la pacification des troubles de l'an M.D. LXVII* (*s.l.*, 1568) p. Diii *verso*.

typical of the rest. One of his more excited accounts, in the
Exhortation, describes how the combatants:

arrachent les enfans des ventres des meres, ou les tuent és berceaux,
violent filles et femmes, gastent païs, bruslent maisons, chasteaux,
bourgs, et villes, destruisent temples, brisent sepultures, rafvissent
biens, s'entrepersecutans inhumainement en tout genre de cruauté,
comme bestes sauvages.

(*Exhortation aux Francois*, pp. 34 *verso*—35 *recto*)

In the *Consideration* he had deplored not only the slaughter, but
the social collapse of a nation:

Nous avons veu toutes les parties de la France en confusion, presque
sans justice, loix et magistrats [. . .]. Nous avons veu batailles et
rencontres donnees, villes assiegees, prinses et saccagees, maisons
pillees, plat païs fourragé, temples demolis, sepultures ruinees, les
rivieres rougies de sang humain, chemins et champs couverts de
personnes cruellement massacrees.

(*Consideration sur l'histoire françoise*, p. 3 *verso*)

These catalogues of disaster have neither the physical ugliness
and 'close-up' horror of Garnier's battle-scenes, nor the pathos
of his laments and prayers for peace. Equally unmoving is Jean
de la Taille's verse description of war and of:

> la perte et la destruction
> Des beaux pays deserts a son occasion;
>
> [. . .] les pleurs, les cris et les voix lamentables
> Des peuples innocens.

(*Œuvres*, IV, p. 123)

But Le Roy, like Garnier, does seem to notice particularly the
devastation of the countryside; the *Exhortation* describes:

les champs paravant laissez en friche, les maisons démeublees, les
villages et bourgs deshabitez.

(*Exhortation*, p. 4 *verso*)

La Madeleyne also speaks of the impoverishment of the countryside, and of how the poorer people carry the heaviest burden

during a war, especially through having to support soldiers and camp followers:

toutes telles oppressions et calamitez tombent de jour en jour sur les pauvres subjects, qui sont contraintz de nourrir et soldats, et goujats, et putains, et outre, ce sont rançonnez et excedez en leurs personnes, et ne s'en faict aucune recherche ou punition [. . .]. A quoy il est tresgrand besoin de remedier et donner ordre, aultrement nous verrons en brief les terres labourables delaissees et abandonnees d'un chacun, et seront les laboureurs contrainctz de quitter leurs maisons par extreme pauvreté.

(*De l'Estat et office d'un bon roy*, pp. 67 *verso*—68 *recto*)

Again, the tone is quite different from Garnier's: we are here in the realm of practical politics, and La Madeleyne offers a practical solution to the problem he describes—make sure that the soldiers are paid.

In short, a number of Garnier's predecessors and contemporaries seem to hold views on war similar to his, or to be concerned with similar aspects of it, and these similarities are not dependent on identical partisan loyalties; but when it comes to the physical horrors of war, or a visual presentation of what it does to a country, Garnier stands quite apart from the others in the violence of his descriptions and the emotional force of his laments.

6

'. . . MAIS LE CRIME EST DE REBELLION'

(*Les Juifves*, Act ii, 654)

I have headed this chapter with a quotation from *Les Juifves* because it alludes to all three closely connected topics which I discuss here as a conclusion to the examination of Garnier's political views. These topics are rebellion, the *clémence/rigueur* debate, and the figure of Nebuchadnezzar. These labels are somewhat arbitrary and unsatisfactory. For instance, there are many kinds of rebellion and sometimes the boundaries between civil war and rebellion are not easy to define (thus Le Roy offers only a distinction between *war*, or fighting between nations, and *sedition*, or fighting within a nation); but the form of rebellion discussed most fully by Garnier is the revolt of a province against a conqueror or king, and this is therefore the kind we shall consider rather than a popular uprising, or the conspiracy of highly placed citizens inspired by ambition, fear or idealism, or the 'palace guard revolt' which killed, for example, the emperor Caligula and obliged Nero to commit suicide. Again, the *clémence/rigueur* debate often arises from or gives rise to a debate on whether a ruler should seek to be loved or feared, and this will also have to be considered here. Finally, the rôle of Nabuchodonosor in *Les Juifves* involves the themes of both *clémence/rigueur* and rebellion, while rebellion may be feared by a ruler as a likely consequence of a wrong decision in the *clémence/rigueur* dilemma, so that my division into three categories is artificial, but necessary for the sake of clarity.

REBELLION

The French Catholics of the sixteenth century saw the Protestants as turbulent and rebellious subjects, disrupting the social order by their seditious tendencies. The religious leaders of the

Protestants however (in opposition, sometimes, to their political leaders), advocated peace and submission. Thus Calvin: 'Que ce vous soit assez d'opposer à leur fureur prières et larmes.' (Aux Fidèles de France, June, 1559) And again:

Puisque nostre debvoir est de souffrir, il nous fault baisser la teste; et puisque Dieu veult que son église soit subjecte à telle condition que tout ainsi qu'une charrue passe sur un champ, que les iniques ayent la vogue pour faire passer leur glaive sur nous depuis un bout jusques à l'autre, ainsi qu'il est dit au pseaulme, que nous ayons les dos apprestez aux coups.
(Aux Fidèles de France, November 1559)[1]

In his letters to Protestant communities, Calvin urged time and again that the Protestants must submit to harsh treatment, and martyrdom if necessary, accepting that their oppressors were the instruments of God, just as Nebuchadnezzar had been allowed by God to ill-treat the Jews. Writing to Coligny after the conspiracy of Amboise, in April, 1561, he deplored the conspiracy and described how he had tried to dissuade restless Protestants from initiating any seditious action.[1]

Théodore de Bèze examined the question of the subject's right to revolt in a meticulously thought-out treatise, *Du Droit des magistrats*.[2] Here he rules that if a sovereign prescribes something contrary to the laws of God, or against his subjects' conscience, they may remonstrate, and even when repeated remonstrances have failed, they still may not initiate direct action against the sovereign, but must ask the protection of a prince of the blood, who alone has sufficient authority to offer resistance to the crown. This provides an explanation of why the Protestants were so anxious to keep Condé and Bourbon as leaders (even if only nominal ones) of their cause.

Thus the Protestants could either argue that they were right to resist because the law they were expected to obey was wicked (to the Catholics such a defence was invalid because they did not consider the law to be unjust), or else, if they respected Théodore de Bèze's ruling, could point to their leaders, indisputably of the

---

1 *Lettres de Jean Calvin*, ed. Jules Bonnet (Paris, 1854) 2 vols., vol. 2, pp. 274, 302.
2 Th. de Bèze, *Du Droit des magistrats sur leurs sujets* (1574).

blood royal. During the minorities of François II and Charles IX they could also claim to be protecting the king's interests against his evil advisers.

The question of obedience to an unjust law or a bad king is discussed by both Protestant and Catholic writers, and the usual Catholic attitude is 'pray for a good prince and put up with the one you have'. In general, Protestants recommend that a 'loi inique' should not be obeyed, but as many are loth openly to counsel rebellion, there is often a certain vagueness as to what form resistance to the law should take. One Catholic who also believes that an unjust law should not be obeyed is more specific as to what to do about it than Protestants such as Nicolas Barnaud: Arnault Sorbin quotes Scripture to reinforce his argument that a man who finds himself required to obey a wicked law has no right to rebel, but only to flee.[1] In the *Excuse aux Nicodemites* Calvin, also, had suggested that the solution to intolerable persecution in France was emigration.

This question, of resisting an unjust or wicked law, arises in Garnier's *Antigone*. It seems clear that Antigone is right to disobey Créon: she embodies 'piété' and must fulfil her duty as Polynice's sister, and as a human being, by burying the dead. On the other hand, Créon is right to punish her, since his duty is to establish order and to execute impartial justice. Thus there is an irreconcilable conflict, not between right and wrong but between two rights. Créon becomes a tyrant, not so much because he made an objectionable law in the first place, as because he is obstinately and excessively harsh in enforcing it, and because he respects neither Antigone's royal lineage, nor Theban public opinion which demands Antigone's release. In this play, Garnier seems to uphold the subject's right to resist an evil injunction (or one which the subject believes to be evil), even while showing that a ruler may be obliged to punish such resistance. The way in which they both claim right on their side is epitomised in two lines from their argument in Act IV:

CRÉON: *Dieu ne commande pas qu'aux loix on n'obeïsse.*
ANTIGONE: *Si fait, quand elles sont si pleines d'injustice.*

(*Antigone*, Act IV, 1808–9)

[1] *Le Vray Resveille-matin* (1576) p. 50.

There is some suggestion from Antigone and Ismène that the conflict between moral duty and the duty of civil obedience is complicated by doubts as to the king's integrity and legitimacy:

ISMÈNE: Mais il a Polynice ennemi declaré.
ANTIGONE: Voire après qu'il s'est veu de son sceptre emparé.
(Act IV, 1610–11)

Ismène is even more outspoken:

> Créon est obey, qui, tyran, voudroit bien
> Déraciner du tout nostre nom ancien.
> (Act IV, 1574)

It is tempting to see this as a Machiavellian interpretation of Créon's behaviour (the new prince exterminating the old ruling family); but when Etéocle and Polynice had killed each other, Créon, as Jocaste's brother, had little choice but to claim the throne, and this attack can be seen as a flash of bitterness at the destruction of Ismène's own family rather than a serious argument against Créon.

Antigone deals with an isolated act of disobedience, not a full-scale rebellion; Antigone does not try to overthrow Créon's authority, although he may feel she threatens it by her insubordination.

The question of rebellion on a larger scale comes into focus in *Les Juifves*. The Jews were a conquered nation, and, what is more, their kings were bound by an oath of loyalty to the conqueror, Nebuchadnezzar. But fretting at their position, the Jews formed an alliance with Nebuchadnezzar's enemy Necho, and in the war which followed Jerusalem was sacked, the Jews were again defeated and brought in captivity to Babylon—Toynbee calls this a classic example of the transportation of a conquered nation, aimed at breaking its spirit. Garnier, in *Les Juifves*, tells only of the fate of the royal household, brought captive to Antioch after an unsuccessful attempt to escape.

In discussing Zedekiah's action (allying with Necho against Nebuchadnezzar) as an example of rebellion, it should be pointed out that by normal standards it need not be considered any such thing. If Zedekiah decided to stop paying tribute to a distant conqueror and form new alliances more favourable to his own people, this seems a fairly reasonable decision for the head of a sovereign state. But Zedekiah's duty to Nebuchadnezzar was imposed on him by God. The Bible uses the word 'rebellion' and so do the characters in *Les Juifves*: so we must accept Garnier's judgment and consider the Jews as rebellious subjects of Nebuchadnezzar. In this play, even more than in *Antigone*, we are shown right and wrong on both sides; it is by no means a simple case of a tyrant bullying a weaker man.

One striking element in the play is that both sides agree that rebellion is a serious crime. Nabuchodonosor refers to Sédécie's rebellion as 'un si vilain outrage' and 'une si detestable et lasche trahison' (Act II, 208, 210). The Jews make no attempt to exculpate themselves, they do not accuse Nabuchodonosor of treating them unjustly, they merely ask for some mercy to be used in the execution of justice. Amital, pleading for Sédécie, does not try to deny either the fact of the crime or its gravity:

LA ROYNE: Vous l'avez outragé.
AMITAL: Il est vray: mais Madame, il en est bien vengé.
                         (Act II, 646–7)

AMITAL: Nous sommes rebellez, voire, je le confesse.
                         (Act II, 655)

She even argues that the greater the crime, the better the opportunity for Nabuchodonosor to show his magnanimity by pardoning it:

> Sire, il est tout certain, le crime d'un suget
> Sert aux bontez d'un Roy d'honorable suget:
> Et plus ce crime est grand que veinqueur il pardonne,
> Et plus en pardonnant de louange il se donne.
>   (Act III, 1013–16)

To sum up: in *Antigone* Garnier shows sympathy for the freedom of the individual conscience; in the sixteenth century this would seem almost a Protestant viewpoint, for Antigone follows her own judgment entirely in deciding where her duty lies and what God requires of her. But at the same time he allows us to respect Créon's need to impose order and to establish himself as a firm and just ruler. In *Les Juifves* the situation is less paradoxical but still involved, in that we are expected to censure Sédécie for his crime of rebellion, while pitying him for the misfortunes that arise from it. These are humane and wise attitudes: the recognition that a dilemma or conflict of duties may be insoluble, and the judgment that condemns the deed while allowing compassion for the doer. The first implies a recognition of the strength of individual conscience more Protestant than Catholic; the second requires a faculty for compassion and tolerance comparable to that of Michel de l'Hospital.

CLÉMENCE/RIGUEUR

Another insoluble dilemma is that which underlies the *clémence/rigueur* debate, and its corollary, the question of whether a king should strive to be loved or feared. As a basis for discussion let us set out briefly the circular argument involved in the love or fear question: if a king seeks to be feared, he may be hated, and if he is hated, he is likely to be assassinated. If he seeks to be loved, he may lose his subjects' respect and be regarded as easy prey for a usurper. The *clémence/rigueur* debate is the same one in slightly different terms: if a prince rules mercifully, his humanity may be mistaken for softness; if he is severe, he may incur his people's hatred. Seneca sums it up in *Octavia*, in the argument between Nero and his tutor:

NERO: Calcat iacentem vulgus.
SENECA: Invisum opprimit.
NERO: Ferrum tuetur principem.
SENECA: Melius fides.
NERO: Decet timeri Caesarem.
SENECA: At plus diligi.
NERO: Metuant necesse est—
SENECA: Quidquid exprimitur grave est.
NERO: Iussisque nostris pareant.
SENECA: Iusta impera—

NERO: Statuam ipse.
SENECA: Quae consensus efficiat rata.
NERO: Respectus ensis faciet.
SENECA: Hoc absit nefas.

(*Octavia*, 455–61)

Many writers raise the question, and in this as in so much else, Machiavelli led the way. In chapter XVII of the *Prince* he discusses first the *clémence/rigueur* aspect and says that:

a prince should not worry if he incurs reproach for his cruelty as long as he keeps his subjects united and loyal. By making an example or two he will prove more compassionate than those who, being too compassionate, allow disorders which lead to murder and rapine. These nearly always harm the whole community, whereas executions ordered by a prince only affect individuals.

(*The Prince*, trans. G. Bull, chapter XVII, p. 95)

This 'be cruel to be kind' theory is neatly paradoxical, and typical of Machiavelli's firm, brisk style of argument. He then goes on to discuss the question whether it is better to be loved or feared:

The answer is that one would like to be both the one and the other; but because it is difficult to combine them, it is far better to be feared than loved if you cannot be both. [. . .] Men worry less about doing an injury to one who makes himself loved than to one who makes himself feared. The bond of love is one which men, wretched creatures that they are, break when it is to their advantage to do so; but fear is strengthened by a dread of punishment which is always effective.

The prince should nonetheless make himself feared in such a way that, if he is not loved, at least he escapes being hated. For fear is quite compatible with an absence of hatred; and the prince can always avoid hatred if he abstains from the property of his subjects and citizens and from their women.

(*Ibid.*, pp. 96–7)

So, on this question of being loved or feared, I conclude that since some men love as they please but fear when the prince pleases, a wise prince should rely on what he controls, not on what he cannot control. He should only endeavour, as I said, to escape being hated.

(*Ibid.*, p. 98)

The recognition that the ideal of being loved *and* feared is impracticable, the rejection of love as a guarantee of loyalty and the matter-of-fact advice on how to escape hatred, are all in keeping with Machiavelli's highly practical approach to statecraft. Such practicality is rare, and few French writers give such a satisfactory answer to the problem. Many simply advise the king to gain his subjects' love (usually by clemency) without working out the possible disadvantages of this. Thus Baïf (in the *Epistre au Roy*) advises Henri III 'sois clément' and tells him to set an example by his own behaviour:

> Ce faisant plus aimé que non pas craint seras.

Saint Thomas, in an unusual and charming extension of the traditional metaphor comparing monarchy to a community of bees, states that the 'king' bee has no sting, or if he has is not allowed to use it (Saint Thomas is not quite sure which is the case).[1] Part of Jean Bodin's long antithetical definition of king and tyrant says that 'l'un est aymé et adoré de tous ses sugets, l'autre les hait touts, et est hay de touts'. (*Republique*, book ii, chapter 4, p. 247). Le Roy in his *Isocrates* works out that the prince should be 'aymé plutost que craint' in an argument remarkable for its abstraction and symmetry, which completely omits to consider any possible dilemma or difficulty in applying this recommendation. (*Trois livres d'Isocrates* (1551) p. 23 *verso*.)

Machiavelli would have dismissed most of these writers as woolly-minded idealists. He might have been equally impatient with a second group, those who claim that the prince does not have to choose between being feared and being loved, since the two are easily reconcilable. Innocent Gentillet, in his attack on Machiavelli which has come to be known as the *Contre-Machiavel*, says that Machiavelli is quite wrong in thinking this combination difficult to achieve; the dilemma is easily resolved by the prince's being loved by the majority of his subjects and feared by the evil-doers.[2] Du Haillan describes the French king as: 'Le Roy,

[1] F. de St. Thomas, *La Vraye forme de bien et heureusement regir* . . . (1569) p. 60. The author states in a dedicatory epistle that this is mainly a compilation, but in a foreword apologizes for being unable to name his sources as he has lost the notebook containing his bibliography.

[2] Gentillet, *Discours, sur les moyens de bien gouverner* . . . (*s.l.*, 1576) p. 376.

qui est Monarque, aimé, reveré, craint et obey', and La Madeleyne asserts that a good king is 'aimé, crainct et honnoré des siens'.[1] Estienne Pasquier goes even further, implying that fear engenders love, saying of the French people's attitude to the kings of France 'le peuple avec une douce crainte a esté induit de les aymer'.[2] Pibrac in his *Quatrains* says the converse when he mentions, with approval, 'craincte qui vient d'amour'.[3] None of these writers investigates the difficulties inherent in what he recommends, and most give the impression of not having spent much thought on the matter.

One point on which they agree is that a tyrannous rule provokes hatred, and that any king other than a tyrant tries to avoid stirring up hatred. Many quote the phrase 'Oderint, dum metuant' as a typical, and repulsive, tyrant's motto.[4] Jean Heluïs quotes it and comments: 'cette voix Tyrannique est mieus seante a quelque Tigre, ou furieus Lion (si nature leur avait ottroié le don de parler) qu'elle n'est à l'homme.' (*Le Miroüer du prince chrétien* (1566) p. 19). But there is no presentation of the state of mind or the type of character which can enjoy this sensation of power and domination, nor even any recognition that a ruler who adhered to the creed of 'oderint, dum metuant' might enjoy a successful, if brief, reign.

Garnier does not offer pious platitudes as readily as some of his contemporaries. In fact his presentation suggests that he is aware of the dilemma inherent in the subject. Once he lets a character offer the 'easy' view that a king should be loved and feared; but when Hémon says this (*Antigone*, Act ıv, 2040), it is part of a bitter argument in which he is trying to put Créon in the wrong; his point is that a king must not violate the 'loi publique' and that if Créon does this he will forfeit the loving respect of his subjects. Hémon is not concerned with the finer points of the relationship between ruler and people, only with

[1] Du Haillan, *De l'Estat et succez des affaires de France* (Paris, 1570) p. 79 *recto*; La Madeleyne, *Discours de l'estat et office d'un bon roy* . . . (Paris, 1575) p. 8.

[2] Pasquier, *Le Pourparler du prince* in *Les Recherches de la France* (Paris, 1660) p. 894.

[3] Pibrac, *Les Quatrains*, 2nd edition (Lyon, 1597) p. 23, quatrain 101.

[4] Cicero, *De Officiis*, ı, 28, 97, quoted from Attius, *Atreus*.

what he considers a gross transgression on his father's part. I believe that Garnier's attitude to the question can be seen more clearly in the discussion on the *clémence/rigueur* theme in *Porcie*, between Octave and Arée. (An equally valid example is the discussion between César (i.e. Octave) and Agrippe in *Marc-Antoine*, Act IV, pp. 220–2.) The discussion in Porcie is modelled on that between Nero and Seneca in *Octavia* (quoted above, pp. 105–6), but it is longer, and Octave is given more reason on his side than Nero. Also, the very exact symmetry of the stichomythia helps to suggest that the arguments are evenly balanced:

ARÉE: La clémence est l'honneur d'un prince débonnaire.
OCTAVE: La rigueur est tousjours aux princes nécessaire.
ARÉE: Un prince est bien voulu pour son humanité.
OCTAVE: Un empereur est craint pour sa sévérité.
ARÉE: Soyez prompt à douceur et tardif à vengeance.
OCTAVE: Mais bien prompt à rigueur et tardif à clémence.
ARÉE: Un prince trop cruel ne dure longuement.
OCTAVE: Un prince trop humain ne règne seurement.
(*Porcie*, Act III, p. 47–8)

Each cites Caesar, Arée praising his clemency, which Octave blames for Caesar's assassination:

ARÉE: César pour se vanger ne proscript jamais homme.
OCTAVE: S'il les eust tous proscripts, il régneroit à Romme.
(*Ibid.*, p. 48)

Thus Octave has some sound practical reasons for his point of view, and this passage exemplifies the way in which Garnier sometimes allows a dilemma to be apparent, without loading the argument so that one side is bound to seem right. In this argument with Arée, we do not feel that it is because he is a tyrant that Octave is advocating harshness rather than mercy, but because he sees it as the more expedient course, and the one more likely to give him a long and secure rule. As Machiavelli says, 'A new prince, of all rulers, finds it impossible to avoid a reputation for cruelty, because of the abundant dangers inherent in a newly won state' (*Prince*, chapter XVII, pp. 95–6), and Octave is in the position of a new prince. On the other hand we are shown elsewhere in the play an Octave with the instincts of a tyrant. One example is his long speech preceding this debate with Arée, when he gloats over his supremacy, and triumphs in the knowledge that the whole Roman world, which means in effect the whole known world:

> Nous sert, nous obéit, nous révère, nous craint.
>
> (*Porcie*, Act III, p. 46)

This presentation of a tyrant's mentality is something which occurs elsewhere, in this play and others, and throws further light on the *clémence/rigueur* problem, as it illustrates some of the characteristics which may accompany, and perhaps explain, the choice of harshness.

We have already discussed the irrelevance of the 'character study' style of criticism to sixteenth-century tragedy. But in the course of his plays Garnier, while using stock characters, does vary them and work out some individual details, so that not one of his tyrants, bereaved women or lovers is quite like the others. In the case of his tyrants, Garnier shows us not so much a series of different men who have one thing in common, namely that they are tyrants, as a series of unmistakable tyrants, but of different kinds; various species, as it were, within the genus Tyrant. *Porcie* provides a particularly good example of this. The whole of Act III would be an irrelevant intrusion if the theme of Porcie's woes, rather than tyrannicide and its consequences, were really intended to be the mainstay of the tragedy. In this act, Garnier is concerned with the triumvirs, showing us the new 'tyrans' of whom we have heard Porcie complain. Two of them, Octave and Marc-Antoine, are shown in some detail, the third, Lépide, being more or less a watered-down version of Octave. When I say 'shown in some detail', let me stress again that there is no question here of a detailed 'character study', no attempt to give 'rounded' pictures of two human beings. Both are examples of a type, the tyrant; but Garnier selects and emphasizes certain details in order to show us two quite different kinds of tyrant.

Octave begins his first long speech (p. 45) by moralizing about the 'traistres' (the conspirators who killed Julius Caesar) and the just punishment they have received for their 'parricide'. But soon this pious pleasure that Caesar is revenged gives way to the exultation of the power-drunk tyrant. 'Maintenant nous régnons' (p. 45)—and Octave glories in ruling, delights in the fact that people tell lies in order to please him:

> monstrant dessus le front
> Pour nous gratifier, autre vouloir qu'ils n'ont.
>
> (Act III, p. 46)

It is commonplace to apply wild beast imagery to tyrants (cf. Jean Heluïs, p. 108 above). Octave, revelling in his tyranny, applies such imagery to himself:

> comme un tygre ireux,
> Qui court opiniastre après un cerf peureux,
> Je roidiray ma course.
>
> (Act III, p. 46)

Marc-Antoine is of a different species. He is the triumphant warrior glorying in his victory. He too uses 'wild' imagery about himself, comparing his military successes to the headlong course of a mountain stream and the angry charge of a bear. He exemplifies two sides of tyranny: the military triumph, and the splendid egotism and self-advertisement, recalling a Marlowe hero. This aspect is perfectly expressed in the speech beginning 'Tout homme volontiers ses ancestres ressent' (pp. 55–6), where he evokes the fame of his ancestor Hercules and claims to be a worthy descendant of that hero. The repetition of 'Moy nay d'un devancier' insists on Antoine's link with Hercules, whose exploits are described rapidly, the pace increasing as the descriptive relative clauses become shorter until they occupy only one line each:

> Qui domta sous ses pieds le sanglier d'Erymante,
> Qui tua desdaigné le fier Théodomante.

After six lines of this catalogue, the pace becomes quicker still, thanks to the sharing of a verb:

> Qui les Centaures durs, genre ixionien,
> Qui Busire inhumain, tyran égyptien,
> Massacra de ses mains.

111

Then comes the climax of the speech—and the climax is Marc-Antoine himself:

> Moy, moy, sorty de luy, que feray-je sinon
> Que tascher d'acquérir un semblable renom . . .

Thus, Octave represents the type of tyrant who delights in the sensation of power, and in the knowledge that he can force other men's wills to comply with his; Marc-Antoine is above all a soldier, with an exuberant delight in his own prowess. He is concerned with his *gloire* and after a resounding victory does not want to bother with the clearing-up operations which Octave cold-bloodedly advises. The idea of hunting down the miserable survivors is repugnant to him. The same distinction is evident when they contemplate their immediate plans and what they will do with the empire which they have divided up between them. Octave and Lépide think of the power they will enjoy, Marc-Antoine's preoccupation is with the battles he will fight:

> LÉPIDE: J'iray, dominateur, où la chaude Cyrène
> En monceaux vagabonds fait jaunir son arène
> Le Libyen farouche, et le Numide pront,
> Le More basané sous ma charge vivront.

> OCTAVE: Je tiendray sous mon joug les belliqueuses Gaules
> Et les rocs Pyrénez aux superbes espaules,
> Avecque leur Espagne, et le subtil Grégeois,
> Veuf de sa liberté, se rendra sous mes lois.

> MARC-ANTOINE: J'empliray de soudars les citez asiennes;
> J'armeray la Syrie et les rives troyennes;
> La Judée, Arabie, heureuses régions,
> Le Pont et l'Arménie auront mes legions;
> J'iray contre le Mède, et sera mon espée
> Dans le sang escoulé de sa gorge trempée.
> Je mettray tout à sac, ne laissant aux maisons
> Que le feu rongera que les rouges tisons.

> (*Porcie*, Act III, p. 64)

Octave and Lépide dream of subduing and dominating (this is emphasized by the repetition of 'sous', as in 'sous ma charge', 'sous mon joug', 'sous mes lois'), Marc-Antoine of fighting, destroying, and commanding great armies.

Other characters in Garnier's plays similarly show certain aspects of the type they embody. Among the tyrant-figures, Pyrrhe displays cruelty and the desire for revenge; Octave in *Marc-Antoine* the *hubris* of a world-conqueror and world-ruler who thinks he controls his own fortune; Créon, the harshness of the new ruler who fears that any display of leniency might be dangerous and encourage others to resist his uncertain authority.

NABUCHODONOSOR

Nabuchodonosor might be said to be all possible kinds of tyrant rolled into one. He is the absolute tyrant. Like Marc-Antoine, he glories in his great armies:

> Je suis environné de mille bataillons
> De soudars indomtez . . .
> (*Les Juifves*, Act II, 194–5)

Like Octave in *Porcie*, he boasts of his rule over many peoples:

> Tous les peuples du monde ou sont de moy sujetz,
> Ou Nature les a delà les mers logez.
> (*Ibid.*, 197–8)

And, like Octave, he takes pleasure in their forced and simulated respect:

LA ROYNE: *Quelle gloire de n'estre honoré que par feinte?*
NABUCHODONOSOR: *Mais c'est une grandeur de l'estre par contreinte.*
> (*Ibid.*, Act III, 915–16)

Like Créon he punishes with particular severity a crime that threatens his own authority:

> *Tous crimes on pardonne*
> *Fors celuy seulement qui touche à la couronne.*
> (*Ibid.*, Act II, 251–2)

Like Octave in *Marc-Antoine* he supposes himself in command of his own fate:

> Dieu fait ce qu'il luy plaist, et moy je fay de mesme.[1]
> (*Ibid.*, Act III, 928)

[1] Cf. Tamburlaine:
I hold the fates bound fast in iron chains
And with my hand turn Fortune's wheel about.
(*1st Tamburlaine*, Act I, 173–4)

But he also has other characteristics, as suggested in the paragraphs dealing with rebellion. It will be useful at this stage to give some idea of the ways in which the political writers use the figure of Nebuchadnezzar. Writers on both sides in the religious debate used biblical quotations to support their arguments. Perhaps Protestants did it somewhat more, while Catholics drew more on the patristic writings, but Protestants certainly did not have a monopoly of biblical quotations. Quotations and references range widely over the whole Bible, but certain figures and episodes recur frequently. Saul is one key figure; he was the first Jewish king (and regarded by many writers as the first king to rule any nation), and he is used to support quite contradictory theories of the origin of kingship. Whether kingship is held to be divine or popular in its origins, the case of Saul can be cited as supporting evidence. Similarly, David can be pointed out either as an example of reverence for kingship because he refrained from killing Saul when Saul was in his power, or, on the contrary, as an example of the subject assuming the right to resist his king, because David fought against Saul. Nebuchadnezzar is another favourite biblical character. Many references to him concern his transformation into a beast; this is cited as a fitting punishment for both his tyranny and his impiety. Other writers refer to his dealings with Daniel, pointing out on the one hand that Daniel was required to pray for Nebuchadnezzar, the evil, heathen king (as were all the Jews), and on the other that Daniel's faith, and his God-given wisdom and courage impressed even the godless tyrant. There are also numerous references to Nebuchadnezzar's treatment of Zedekiah, the 'Sédécie' of *Les Juifves*.

Starting with a Protestant writer, we find numerous references to Nebuchadnezzar in Calvin's *Institution*. In book I, chapter xvii (1560 edition) is a theological argument on the subject 'Que Dieu se sert tellement des meschans [. . .] que toutesfois il demeure pur de toute tache et macule'; here, Calvin takes Nebuchadnezzar as an example of a wicked man being used by God while God remains untainted by the wickedness of his unknowing agent. Another relevant passage is in book IV, chapter xx ('Du Gouvernement civil'), section 25, where Calvin states that the Lord requires men to show respect to their rulers, good or bad: 'Les iniques sont là pour punir les iniquités du peuple'. In the following section (26) he illustrates this by referring to Nebuchadnezzar and his treatment of the Jews.

Turning to other Protestant writers, we find that De Bèze mentions Nebuchadnezzar and Zedekiah in *Du Droit des magistrats*.[1] He distinguishes between a ruler issuing ungodly commands, which ought not to be obeyed (p. 737), and one who is merely harsh, and should not be resisted as resistance would be a violation of the double contract, binding king and people to God, and to each other (p. 759). Giving an instance of wrongful resistance to a harsh ruler, he says: 'les circonstances condamnent entierement la revolte, et le parjure, de Sedechias et des siens' (p. 781); and he reminds us that God ordered the Jews to pray for Nebuchadnezzar.

Another Protestant, the anonymous author of a pamphlet reprinted in the *Memoires de Condé*, lists 'Sedechias' along with 'Nabuchodonosor' among tyrants who have perished violently or miserably.[2]

Zedekiah is the king of whom the Bible says:

> He did that which was evil in the sight of the Lord his God, and humbled not himself before Jeremiah, a prophet speaking from the mouth of the Lord. And he also rebelled against King Nebuchadnezzar, who had made him swear by God: but he stiffened his neck, and hardened his heart from turning unto the Lord God of Israel.
>
> (*II Chronicles*, chapter 36, verses 12–13)

Garnier does not present Zedekiah as a man who could reasonably be called a tyrant, as he is by the anonymous Huguenot pamphleteer; but although in contrast to Nebuchadnezzar he embodies an idea of Christian kingship, Sédécie is guilty of two faults: of breaking his oath to Nebuchadnezzar, and of involving his people in this futile and disastrous escapade. Both of these

[1] Page references are to *Memoires de l'estat de France sous Charles IX* (Meidelbourg, 1577), in which this treatise was reprinted (vol. 2, pp. 735–790).

[2] *Sentences redoutables, et arrest rigoureux du jugement de Dieu, à l'encontre de l'impieté des Tyrans, recueillies tant des Saintes Escritures comme de toutes autres histoires* (Lyon, 1564) reprinted in *Memoires de Condé* (London and Paris, 1743) vol. v, pp. 56–65.

might be loosely described as 'political' faults, whereas the Bible places more emphasis on the question of impiety.

Catholic writers also use the figure of Nebuchadnezzar to illustrate their arguments, but their main interest seems to be not in Zedekiah's position but in Nebuchadnezzar's as the unwitting instrument of God. Thus Michel de l'Hospital cites the Babylonians as an example when he says that the wicked are sometimes allowed to prosper in order to be the 'fléaux' of God's vengeance.[1] Arnault Sorbin takes this one step further when he says that Nebuchadnezzar was destroyed because he was unaware that his power came from God and that he was in fact being used by God.[2] Claude d'Albon has the same view, and both he and Sorbin point out that Nebuchadnezzar in spite of his wickedness was called 'le serviteur de Dieu' and acknowledged as such by God; this is the closest they come to the Zedekiah story.[3]

It is interesting that when political writers use the story of Nebuchadnezzar the tendency is for Protestants to point out the guilt of Zedekiah in rebelling against Nebuchadnezzar, and for Catholics to emphasize that Nebuchadnezzar was an infidel and a blasphemer, although he was at the same time being used by God, and allowed by God to enjoy the privilege of kingship. There is one Catholic writer who combines the two aspects. Jean Bodin believes that no subject has the right to take any action, either 'par voye de justice' or 'par voye de fait' against a truly sovereign monarch (the true mark of sovereignty being the power to legislate). Therefore Zedekiah was in the wrong; and to emphasize the rigour of this judgment, Bodin gives a long description of Nebuchadnezzar's infamous conduct before concluding: 'Et neantmoins nous voyons le Prophete Ezechiel irrité contre Sedechie Roy de Hierusalem, detester bien fort sa perfidie, deloyauté et rebellion contre son Roy Nabuchodonosor, et qu'il ne meritoit rien moins que la mort'. (*République*, book II, chapter 5, pp. 257–8)

Nebuchadnezzar was destructive, cruel, vindictive and blas-

---

[1] M. de l'Hospital, *Discours sur la pacification des troubles de l'an M.D. LXVII* (1568) p. A ii *verso*.

[2] A. Sorbin, *Le Vray Resveille-matin* (1576) p. 42 *verso*.

[3] Cl. d'Albon, *De la Majesté royalle* (1575) p. 9 *verso*, p. 13 *recto*.

phemous; yet he was the servant of God, and Zedekiah wronged him, and was a false vassal, a rebellious subject. That is Bodin's verdict, and it agrees so closely with Garnier's that it seems reasonable to point to Bodin's work for a straightforward political exposition of what Garnier presents dramatically in *Les Juifves*. Bodin and some Protestant writers certainly come closer to Garnier on this point than most Catholic writers.

But Garnier has more to say about Nebuchadnezzar and the Jews than Bodin can say in one paragraph. What does he add to his historical data? Apart from the style in which he expresses these events Garnier makes, I think, two main additions, one to the figure of Nebuchadnezzar, one to the play as a whole.

The addition to Nebuchadnezzar is a characteristic which becomes apparent in the scene between Nabuchodonosor and the Jewish women led by Amital. In this scene, Nabuchodonosor responds to Amital's pleading on Sédécie's behalf by appearing to relent and promise mercy; but the form of words he uses is ambiguous:

NABUCHODONOSOR: Bien que sa forfaiture ait la mort desservie,
  Pour le respect de vous je luy laisse la vie.
AMITAL: Que les fers il ne porte, affranchi desormais.
NABUCHODONOSOR: Devant qu'il soit une heure il n'en verra jamais.
AMITAL: O suprème bonté! que vos genoux j'embrasse,
  Je ne merite pas recevoir telle grace.
  [. . .]
LES ROYNES: Prenez de ces enfans quelque solicitude.
NABUCHODONOSOR: Je les affranchiray du joug de servitude,
  Et de tous les malheurs qui chetivent un Roy
  Sous la main de celuy qui luy donne la loy.
                              (Act III, 1191–6, 1199–202)

Amital accepts the king's apparent change of heart; and only in the last scene but one of the play do the Jewish queens and she realize the sinister ambiguity:

  Hé cruel! tu disois que le Roy ne mourroit,
  Et que jamais, captif, Babylon ne verroit:
  O que tu disois vray! car jamais de sa veuë
  Ne sera Babylon ny autre cité veuë.
                      (Act V, 2045–8, Les Roynes)

This deception of Amital by Nabuchodonosor has been called 'Machiavellian'. It is so only in a certain literary sense, the sense in which the craftier villains of Elizabethan tragedy are described as Machiavellian. This use reflects the English (and French) view of Machiavelli in the sixteenth century, as a guileful, dishonest and thoroughly evil mind: 'a sort of rallying point for whatever was most loathsome in statecraft, and indeed in human nature at large', as Mario Praz puts it.[1] The 'Machiavellian' characters in Elizabethan tragedy are those who destroy their enemies by means of devious plots, or by 'Italian' methods such as poison. This is of course a misrepresentation of Machiavellian theory. Machiavelli does permit, indeed commend, the use of deceit and ruse in the service of the state, or to gain political ends (see the famous passage in which he says that the prince needs the combined qualities of the lion and the fox, *Prince*, chapter xviii). The 'Machiavellian' characters in English tragedy normally exercise their ingenuity and malice on private revenges (like Flaminio in Webster's *White Devil*). Nabuchodonosor's use of deception is equally trivial, and un-Machiavellian in the true sense, in that it does not gain him any political advantage—he needs none. The only result of his words is to give some brief and illusory comfort to Amital and the Jewish women, and to increase his own triumph over them. Not only is it un-Machiavellian in being un-political and achieving nothing positive, but also it is not a ruse or plot but an equivocation, a play on words; it is comparable to the equally misleading words of the witches in *Macbeth* when they inspire Macbeth with ill-founded confidence by their assurance that no 'man of woman born' can hurt him, or even to the verbal juggling used by a good character in *The Merchant of Venice* when Portia argues in court that the pound of flesh due to Shylock must not contain 'one drop of Christian blood'. A more relevant comparison is with Seneca, for it should be pointed out that this verbal trick played by Nabuchodonosor is similar to the grim joke made by Atreus to his brother Thyestes, who has just eaten his own children (killed

---

[1] 'The politic brain: Machiavelli and the Elizabethans', reprinted in *The Flaming Heart*, p. 58.

and cooked by Atreus):

> Hic esse natos crede in amplexu patris;
> hic sunt eruntque; nulla pars prolis tuae
> tibi subtrahetur. ora quae exoptas dabo
> totumque turba iam sua implebo patrem.
> satiaberis, ne metue.
>
> (*Thyestes*, 976–80)

Thus Nabuchodonosor's sinister jest with Amital does not alter our picture of him as a type-character whose origins are Senecan. What does modify this picture is that Senecan tyrants are completely evil and in the wrong, whereas Nabuchodonosor has a legitimate grievance against Sédécie, and has the authority to punish him; he even at times seems to display some unvillainous tendencies such as a moment of respect or pity when he says to the kneeling Amital:

> Levez-vous, je ne veux que vous soyez ainsi.
>
> (Act III, 1009)

If Nabuchodonosor's deception of Amital is a Senecan addition to the figure of Nebuchadnezzar as Garnier found him in biblical and historical sources (an addition in keeping with the principle of *contaminatio*), the other addition is something which is not to be found in Seneca. Nabuchodonosor's words to Amital have often been described as producing an effect of dramatic or tragic irony, since we, the readers, guess that Amital is mistaken in her interpretation of them. But this is irony of a very simple, even crude, kind; it is similar to that used by Seneca in *Thyestes* when, after the description of the murder of Thyestes's children, we are shown Thyestes trying to cheer himself up and wondering what foreboding prevents him from enjoying his new happiness at the reconciliation with his brother Atreus (*Thyestes*, 920 ff.). *Les Juifves* contains much subtler and more serious effects of irony than this, arising from the whole subject of the play, implicit in any prose account of the story but made more evident and forceful by a dramatic representation.

There are three levels of irony in *Les Juifves*. First, the Jews are in the wrong; but Nabuchodonosor, who is punishing them, is blasphemous, arrogant, cruel, vindictive: a most unlikely instrument, it would seem, of the wrath of God. Secondly, there is irony in the fact that the Jews are being punished because God loves them; Michel de l'Hospital has a comment which is highly relevant here:

Et en Ezéchiel, le Seigneur adressant des parolles pleines de reproches à la ville de Hiérusalem: *Jam, inquit, non irascar tibi; zelus meus recessit a te.* 'Je ne me courrouceray contre toy, a dict le Seigneur, car je ne t'aime plus.' N'estre plus aimé de Dieu! ne sentir plus de verges sur nostre dos! quelle plus grande malédiction nous peult il arriver?[1]

This gives as it were the philosophical or theological reconciliation of the situation in *Les Juifves*; but dramatically, it remains ironic, especially as the punishment which the Jews receive, a sign of God's love for them, is so severe that they feel abandoned by God. The final level of irony is that Nabuchodonosor is punishing them for rebellion but God, through Nabuchodonosor, is punishing them for impiety. Sédécie is aware of this:

> C'est pour avoir peché devant ta sainte face,
> O pere, et n'avoir craint le son de ta menace:
> Te reputant semblable à ces Dieux que lon fond,
> Ou qu'en pierre et en bois les statuaires font,
> Qui n'ont ame ny force, abominable ouvrage,
> Aux hommes abestis qui leur vont faire hommage.
> J'ay failli, j'ay peché . . .
>
> (Act iv, 1287–93)

His consciousness of being guilty of another crime than that for which he is being punished almost seems to anticipate Schillerian tragedy; Johanna in *Die Jungfrau von Orléans* allows herself to be condemned for witchcraft because she bears the guilt of her love for La Hire; Maria in *Maria Stuart* accepts the death sentence for a conspiracy in which she had no part, because she is conscious of deserving punishment for her part in the murder of her second husband, Darnley. The comparison is not exact, of course, because Sédécie is guilty of both the crime which weighs

---

[1] *Traité de la réformation de la justice*, in *Œuvres inédites de Michel de l'Hospital, chancelier de France*, ed. P. J. S. Dufey, 2 vols. (Paris, 1825) vol. 2, 5e partie, p. 42.

on his own conscience (blasphemy) and the one for which he is ostensibly being punished (rebellion). Sédécie is fully aware of the double punishment, and of the difference between Nabuchodonosor's complaint against the Jews, and God's; the rest of the Jews are not fully aware of this, and Nabuchodonosor has no notion of it at all, which is one reason why he too will eventually be punished, for he does not recognize the source of his power, nor realize why the Jews were allowed to fall into his clutches.

The end of the play is in some sense a resolution of these ironies, and a compromise; it does not alter the present plight of the Jews (for we, and they, must accept that they deserve punishment), nor offer more than a promise of Nabuchodonosor's downfall; but to make the Jews' sufferings slightly more bearable, and to allow us to know of God's ultimate justice, we must be told that Nabuchodonosor is to be punished in due course, and that the torment of the exiled and enslaved Jews will not last for ever. The prophecies in the last scene give us that assurance.

This examination of Garnier's treatment of the themes of rebellion, *clémence* and *rigueur*, and the figure of King Nebuchadnezzar leads to the conclusion that he does not always follow conventional Catholic and royalist lines on vexed questions, that he is honest enough to present an insoluble dilemma in terms which show how evenly balanced the arguments may be for both sides, and that in a play whose most conspicuous and memorable characters are stock figures (Nabuchodonosor and Amital), he can produce strong and disturbing effects of irony.

7

THE TRAGIC DISCOURSE

What sort of political tragedies did Garnier write? That is, what makes them different from other plays of the time with obvious political intentions or with some political elements? How are the political elements incorporated into the tragedies? Are all the tragedies political to the same extent and in the same way?

These questions obviously entail comparison, but since the number of plays which could be brought into the discussion is very large, I shall select only a few of these for quotation or detailed examination, mentioning others only very briefly. A strong family resemblance marks many sixteenth-century classical tragedies and abundant quotation would be wearisome, especially since a great many of the plays written in the sixteenth century (as in later centuries) are, at best, mediocre.

There are obviously various kinds of plays which can be called 'political' and we must look at several kinds in order to see clearly where Garnier's strength and originality lie.

The most completely and unsubtly political plays are those which one might describe as polemical, dealing directly with current events in France, using either the real names of the people involved or fictitious names which do not conceal identity in the slightest.

I shall describe three examples of this kind, representing different points of view and employing different techniques.

The earliest of the three is Chantelouve's *Tragedie de feu Gaspar de Colligni*, published in 1575.[1] Apart from one note-

---

[1] François de Chantelouve, *La Tragedie de feu Gaspar de Colligni jadis Admiral de France, contenant ce qui advint à Paris le 24 Aoust 1572, avec le nom des personnages* (*s.l.*, 1575). Quoted here in the eighteenth century edition in the Bibliothèque Nationale (Yf. 6359).

worthy stage direction—'Ici, d'Andelot retourne aux Enfers'—
this play is chiefly interesting as an attempt to combine some
elements of classical drama with modern events and characters.
Thus there is a chorus, 'le peuple François', which duly performs
at the end of each act. The god Mercury is one of the characters,
and there are also some Furies who accompany D'Andelot when
he emerges from Hell. The play has five acts, and there is some
imitation of classical literature, as when the chorus at the end of
Act I opens with a paraphrase of Horace's 'Integer vitae,
scelerisque purus', before returning to abuse of Admiral de
Coligny (pp. 12–17). The political bias is evident from the start:
this is an attempt to vindicate Charles IX's part in the Massacre
of St Bartholomew, chiefly by blackening the character of
Coligny, who must in fact have been one of the very few completely honest, patriotic and admirable leaders on either side.
Here he is shown as thoroughly unscrupulous, hypocritical and
ambitious:

> Toute religion désormais je renonce,
> Voire, je quitterois celle que Beze annonce
> S'il ne falloit masquer d'ombre de pieté,
> Ce que j'ai entreprins contre la Royauté :
> [. . .]   et fuyant toute Loi,
> Qui veuille retenir ma main sous son empire,
> Moy seul exempt de Loi, estre Roy je désire.
>
> (Act I, p. 5)

Charles IX expresses a kind of patriotic and kingly anguish over
the civil war:

> Car en tous ces combats des serviteurs fidelles
> J'ai fait perte, en perdant les mutins et rebelles,
> Et lesquels en perdant, quoique rebelles sont,
> De pitié toutesfois ma poitrine se rompt . . .
>
> (Act II, p. 20)

He also takes the side of mercy in a *clémence/rigueur* debate with
a composite character representing 'le Conseil du Roy'. One
point of interest in the form of this debate is that the rhyme
straddles the stichomythic couplets instead of fitting into their
pattern:

LE ROY: Mais quoi! miséricorde est agréable à Dieu.

LE CONSEIL: Mais justice lui est beaucoup plus agréable.

LE ROY: Pardonner l'ennemi fut toujours bien louable.

LE CONSEIL: Chastier les meschans fut toujours grand vertu.

(Act v, p. 45)

This is unusual; in most examples of rhyming stichomythia each rhymed couplet is one 'thrust and parry' in the duel of words. The effect of this unusual pattern is odd and disturbing.

It is plain that the political 'message' of this play is a propaganda message: Coligny was an ambitious rogue, Charles IX a tender-hearted idealist. Other polemical plays shout equally loudly; one, *La Guisiade*, proclaims a point of view which its author later abandoned.[1] Pierre Matthieu, a Ligueur when he wrote this play, later became a royalist, and was reconciled to Henri IV, who even appointed him official 'historiographe de France'. The violently partisan *Guisiade* recounts 'le massacre du duc de Guise'. Among the characters is a composite personage referred to only as 'le N.N.'. This sinister figure represents those Frenchmen misguided enough to support Henri III, with whose names, says Matthieu, he does not wish to soil his poem. Henri III is over-tolerant of the infidel, the heretic and 'le Machiaveliste', he listens to evil counsellors (such as 'le N.N.'), does not trust his irreproachable subject, the Duc de Guise, is weak, vacillating and a religious hypocrite. Guise is trusting, upright, loves his King and his God, and believes in the King's friendliness until he is caught in the trap at Blois. This play, like *Gaspar de Colligni*, contains some elements of classical tragedy such as the use of a chorus and of rhetorical developments based on commonplaces; even the structure of this play is to some extent classical, for example the last act shows Madame de Nemours, mother of the Duc de Guise, being told of his death—a scene which is almost obligatory in sixteenth-century tragedy.

As a last example of polemic drama, I shall mention *Cléophon*, by J. de Fonteny.[2] In true classical style, the first act consists of

---

[1] Pierre de Matthieu, *La Guisiade* (Lyon, 1589).

[2] *Cléophon, tragédie conforme et semblable à celles que la France a veues durant les guerres civilles*, par J. D. F. (Paris, 1600).

a monologue by Mégère, followed by a chorus. The other characters have 'classical' names which do not conceal their identity; Cléophon is Henri III, Apliste is the Ligue, Stasiode the city of Paris; Taraptan, Palamnaise, Diadotime are the names given to Mayenne, Jacques Clément and Catherine de Médicis.

This play contains many commonplace meditations and discussions, some of them political; it is not without a certain elegance of expression, and Fonteny pleasingly varies the tone of his writing, moving with ease from an explosive shout to a murmur. Thus towards the end of the play after Cléophon has been assassinated, Thrasie (Henri IV) brings the scene of violence and horror to a quiet close with a gentle description of the shepherd's happy life, neatly comparing the attributes of shepherd and king:

> Ayant pour seigneurie un petit champ rural,
> Ayant pour sceptre en main une croche houllette,
> Pour couronne un chappeau que le volleur n'appette,
> Pour sa garde un bon chien, pour peuple ses agneaux,
> Qui luy donnent par an certains tributs nouveaux
> De leur molle toison . . .
>
> (Act v, p. 42)

Like the *Guisiade* and *Gaspar de Colligni*, this play is strongly partisan; this time the bias is in favour of Henri III, showing him as the embodiment of mercy and goodness, while the Ligue tries to poison his mother's mind with evil advice.

There is obviously little similarity between these plays with their strong partisanship, and Garnier's, containing a general political creed which does not exactly tally with any one body of political opinion. All they have in common is a certain number of commonplace themes and some direct imitation; thus Diadotime addresses Fortune in Act III of *Cléophon* in words that seem to echo Hécube's opening speech in *La Troade*:

> Le Mal faict t'est commun, le bien t'est odieux,
> Qui le voudra sçavoir me vienne voir chetive,
> Qu'il jette l'oeil sur moy, il me verra captive.
>
> (*Cléophon*, Act III, p. 19)

There is a second kind of 'propaganda' play which is sectarian rather than partisan: that is, a play with a biblical or apocryphal subject, presenting a distinct doctrinal theme. There are many plays in this category, particularly by Protestants. Extreme examples are the plays by Théodore de Bèze (*Abraham sacrifiant*) and Louis Desmasures (*Tragedies sainctes*, a trilogy on the life of David), which celebrate various moral qualities such as submission to the will of God, faith and humility, and have a strong Protestant bias. Not all biblical plays are so straightforwardly propagandist and sectarian as those of Théodore de Bèze and Louis Desmasures. For example, the work of George Buchanan and Jean de la Taille, although coloured by their religious concerns, is certainly less explicitly denominational.

Buchanan's two tragedies are *Jephthes, sive votum*, and *Baptistes, sive calumnia* (which may allude to the life and death of Sir Thomas More). Buchanan was a stylist in Latin, and Florent Chrestien in his 1567 translation of *Jephthes* manages to reproduce some of Buchanan's crispness and elegance, so that thanks to one of his translators (Vesel's version is much more clumsy), the Scottish Buchanan can claim some standing as a contributor to French vernacular tragedy. *Jephthes* is a straightforward narration of Jephtha's vow and its consequences; the intellectual kernel of the work is a long scene of dialogue between Jephtha and the priest where the arguments are very evenly balanced on either side: the priest adopts a tone of sweet reasonableness as he argues that it cannot be right for Jephtha to do anything so barbarous as sacrifice his daughter; the 'Protestant' Jephtha sticks doggedly to his view of 'simple et sotte vérité'—that he is bound by his solemn oath. Thus the priest is on the side of humanity and a certain degree of 'souplesse', while Jephtha thinks the priest's arguments are casuistical, and is uncompromising and literal in his own conception of duty. Jephtha carries out his oath, but the reader is left not entirely certain that he was right to do so. *Baptistes* is both more religious and more political than *Jephthes*. The reader's or spectator's sympathy for the martyr Johannes, continuing to witness to his faith in spite of threats, slander and the machinations of evil men in high places, is intended to encourage religious zeal, particularly in James VI of Scotland (later James I of England) to whom the play is dedicated. At the same time there is a political element involved, in the figure of Herod and his speeches about tyranny, the identification of a king with his subjects, the ethics of kingship. I have discussed elsewhere (chapter 2, p. 20) the ironic twist which Buchanan adds to the play by the discrepancy between Herod's public utterances and private thoughts. The only point I wish to make here is that these words are used only to show more ingeniously the crooked workings of a tyrant's mind. Herod's political speeches are relevant to the plot, and his political involvement is central to the play; but at the same time Buchanan has no genuinely political message, he is not 'saying' anything about kingship except that Herod is a wicked king. Yet the play is intended to be didactic. On the religious level, it glorifies true religion, and ends with a meditation on immortal life. On the political level, the victory goes to slander, hypocrisy and absolutism. The aims expressed by Buchanan in his preface are to teach a religious lesson, and to warn James VI not to become a tyrant; but the only argument offered against tyranny is a moral one, since in practical terms, tyranny and calumny are successful in the play.

Kingship is the subject of such political speeches as occur in Jean de la Taille's *Saül le furieux* (which contains more political elements than La Taille's other tragedy, *La Famine, ou les Gabeonites*). In chapter 2 (p. 21) I pointed out that La Taille makes more use of the royal rank of his characters than does Seneca, and that Saül's kingship is a central element in the play. In that sense, then, La Taille's *Saül* is more political than any of Seneca's tragedies. Another political element in the play is praise of patriotism, but the main political themes centre on Saül's burden of kingship, his feeling that he has involved his people in ruin and that his guilt brings a 'desastre universel' (line 903) on Israel, because God is quite prepared to harass the whole of Palestine in order to bring about the destruction of Saül.[1] We have discussed earlier the *clémence/rigueur*, 'revenge

[1] Quotations and line references from A. Werner's edition (*Jean de la Taille und sein 'Saül le furieux'*) in *Münchener Beiträge zur romanischen und englischen Philologie*, XL, 1908

or mercy' arguments which are common in Seneca, in Garnier and in other sixteenth century writers.[1] We saw that in Garnier the usual implication is that the question involved is insoluble since a harsh prince is hated and resisted, a mild one despised as weak. But on the whole our sympathy (even if not our intellectual agreement) is allowed to be with the advocate of mildness. In La Taille's play, Saül is shown to have been on the side of mercy, and to have behaved as a humane and generous conqueror:

> Tout ne fut mis à sac, ains par grand courtoisie
> Au triste Roy Agag vous laissastes la vie,
> Plustost que de souiller dedans son sang vos mains.
> (Act ii, 309–11)

It is for this act of 'grand courtoisie' that Saül is now condemned. Not unnaturally, he is repelled by the 'inhumanity' of God:

> O que sa Providence est cachee aux humains!
> Pour estre donc humain j'esprouve sa cholere,
> Et pour estre cruel il m'est donc debonnaire!
> Hé Sire, Sire, lás! Fault il donc qu'un vainqueur
> Plustost que de pitié use fier de rigueur?
> [. . .]
> Vault il pas mieulx avoir
> Esgard à quelque honneur, qu'à nostre grand pouvoir?
> (Act ii, 312 ff.)

There is a danger here that the audience may be too much on Saül's side: even the author's preface says that Saül omitted to carry out instructions 'par mesgarde, ou par quelque raison humaine', which does not seem very incriminating (in the biblical account, *I Samuel* 15, Saul says he did it 'because I feared the people, and obeyed their voice', so that he appears slightly more guilty there than in La Taille's version); furthermore, in the play Saül rouses pity by his despair and indecision:

> J'ay l'esprit si confus d'horeur, de soing, d'effroy,

[1] Other examples in dramatic literature include an argument about 'douceur' and 'force' between Marc-Antoine and César in Jacques Grévin's *César* (Act i) and a similar argument between Herod and Herodias in George Buchanan's *Baptistes* (2nd episode).

Que je ne puis resoudre aucun advis en moy.

(Act ii, 447–8)

He also provokes admiration by his heroism at the end, praised by the Second Escuyer and by David:

O Roy tu monstres bien ton cueur estre heroique.

(Act iv, 1099)

Tu fus, ô Roy, si vaillant et si fort
Qu'autre que toy ne t'eust sceu mettre à mort.

(Act v, 1499–1500)

This fits well enough with La Taille's view (as explained in the *Art de la tragédie*) that the aim of tragedy must be 'd'esmouvoir et de poindre merveilleusement les affections d'un chascun', and that it should not be about 'Seigneurs extremement meschants, et que pour leurs crimes horribles ils meritassent punition'; but La Taille must prevent Saül from seeming too unjustly treated; we need to be reminded of his guilt, and this is done through warnings and reproaches from several of the other characters. Thus the Escuyer points out that Saül's mercy to Agag was:

contre le vouloir
Que Dieu par Samuel vous fit ainsi sçavoir.

(Act v, 1307–8)

Samuel's spirit enlarges on the same theme (Act iii, 773–6), and the chorus of Levites also mentions Saül's responsibility for the curse that has struck Israel. Thus the first of his noble deeds (sparing Agag) is seen as impious and having disastrous consequences; and later his heroic decision to enter the battle is also criticized by the Levites (Act iv, 1119–25). He is further incriminated by his dealings with the witch of Endor, about which he is warned by the Escuyer (Act ii, 462, Act iii, 691) and by the Levites (chorus, end of Act ii). Throughout the scene with the witch runs the feeling that an evil business is being undertaken; this impression is enhanced by the uncouth mixture of mythologies (probably less startling to a sixteenth-century hearer than to a modern one) in the 'Phitonisse's' invocation, as when she describes Lucifer's fall:

Tous tous je vous appelle: et vous Anges encore

129

Que l'arrogance fit avecques Lucifer
Culbuter de l'Olympe au parfond de l'enfer.

(Act III, 642–4)

In fact, Saül is put firmly in the wrong throughout the play, so that one might call this play in a sense anti-political: it is not only preaching a moral of pious resignation (as Théodore de Bèze does in *Abraham sacrifiant*) but saying that the virtues of heroism and generosity (virtues of a good king) are not enough to outweigh the sin of disobedience to the word of God. This is the moral lesson of the play, together with the more familiar one to be derived from the edifying spectacle of a great and proud monarch reduced to defeat and despair by the 'effects de Fortune maligne' or the 'inconstances de la Fortune', as La Taille refers to them in the dedicatory sonnet to Henri de Navarre and in the *Art de la tragédie* respectively.

It is perhaps not too far-fetched to carry this one stage further, and suggest that this 'anti-political' strain may represent a Protestant political attitude. If one translates the situation into human terms, putting king and subject in the place of God and Saül, the lesson that emerges is that a subject has not the right to rebel even when he disapproves of the orders he is given and feels that he has a legitimate grievance (the story of Jonah would provide another illustration of the same predicament). Thus one can say either that the play is political in a negative sense because it attacks certain political values, or that it may, with its emphasis on obedience and patient endurance, express the political views of Protestant leaders, as set out for example by Calvin in 1561 (the year in which, according to his German editor, La Taille probably began the composition of Saül[1]):

Or combien que la tristesse nous soit commune avec tous, si nous fault-il restraindre et tenir en bride, et donner tel conseil l'un à l'autre que celuy qui a toute authorité par devers nous soit simplement obéi [. . .]. Toute nostre sagesse est de prattiquer la leçon que nous a apprise le souverain Maistre, assavoir de posseder nos vies en patience.

(*Lettres de J. Calvin*, p. 392–3, à l'église d'Aix, le 1er mai 1561)

---

[1] A. Werner, *Jean de la Taille und sein 'Saül le furieux'*, p. xxi.

So far, we have not found any plays similar to Garnier's, either in the quantity of political matter they contain, or the political attitudes they seem to advocate. Buchanan's and La Taille's plays have a lesson, but they give it by being exemplary tales; this is not Garnier's method.

There are other plays that are in some respects more similar to Garnier's than those we have already discussed, in that they present a classical or religious theme in a classical form, and contain some references to political topics, usually of the commonplace type. Almost any French tragedy of the latter half of the sixteenth century might claim to come in this category, which includes plays by Toutain, Filleul, Jodelle, Guersens, La Peruse, Roillet, Chantelouve, Rivaudeau, Grévin and Montchrestien. One of them, the *Aman* of the Protestant writer André de Rivaudeau, treats its subject in a way that gives it some similarity to Garnier's *Juifves* (in both, a timid young queen pleads with her mighty husband to spare the Jewish people) and Garnier has indeed imitated some passages from Rivaudeau's play (published in 1566).[1] It is more worth imitating than many, for the verse is vigorous and fluent. Aman has an arrogance worthy of Nabuchodonosor:

> Je n'ay que faire aux Dieux, car ma grande puissance
> Me promet à part moy la fin de ma vengeance.
> (Act I, p. 70)[2]

The entrance of Esther in Act II is plainly the model for the first appearance of Nabuchodonosor's queen in *Les Juifves*, with Esther's greeting to the sun, and the sudden feeling of youth and hope contrasting with a preceding atmosphere of depressing gloom. There are other parallels, and so many references to the story of Zedekiah (whom Rivaudeau, like Garnier, calls Sédécie, whereas most sixteenth-century writers call him Sédéchias), that one wonders whether it was this play which suggested the theme of *Les Juifves* to Garnier. But apart from one passage in a

[1] The play is summarized and studied by R. Lebègue in *La Tragédie française de la Renaissance*, pp. 379–96.

[2] Page references are to *Les Œuvres poétiques d'André de Rivaudeau, gentilhomme de Bas Poitou*, ed. C. Mourain de Sourdeval (Paris, 1859) in which *Aman* occupies pp. 53–132.

very long chorus (end of Act II) where it is pointed out that tyrants can be used by God to punish his erring people, there is little political thought in the tragedy, so that in that respect Garnier does not imitate Rivaudeau.

There is one author in sixteenth-century France who is frequently referred to as Garnier's 'disciple', although such a description can mean little more than that he imitated Garnier's style in some respects. There was no personal contact between Garnier, the provincial lawyer, Catholic and loyalist, and Antoine de Montchrestien, the adventurer who was executed as a Protestant rebel. Montchrestien's style is certainly as rich as Garnier's, his subjects are ones which Garnier might well have chosen. Yet there is a vast difference between the two dramatists. The heart of the difference is in the way in which they use their elaborate, patterned language, particularly when dealing with cruelty or grief.

In the chapter on war (chapter 5) it was emphasized that Garnier frequently describes the horrors, the suffering and the desolation of war. Montchrestien also has a number of passages relating gruesome events. How do such passages differ from Garnier's? One difference is that Garnier attacks all the senses: his descriptions are not only visual, they evoke smells, sounds, tactile sensations; he batters all our senses so that the impression is inescapable (see, e.g., the battle descriptions in *Porcie* and *Cornélie*). Montchrestien relies more on the visual element alone to achieve his effects. A further, and more important difference is that Garnier describes physical pain in such a way as to rouse pity. He gives specific details to describe the pain, he uses pathetic diminutives and words like 'pauvre'. A good example is the passage describing the treatment of the Jewish princes and children at the end of *Les Juifves*. The princes come into the arena bound in pairs, unkempt, dirty:

> Leur dos courbé plioit sous le servile poix
> Des chaines qui serroyent leurs bras couchez en croix,
> Les jambes leur enfloyent sous les fers escorchees . . .
> (Act v, 1905–7)

Then the children appear, and meet Sédécie:

Les pauvres Enfantets avec leurs dois menus
Se pendent à son col et à ses bras charnus . . .

(Act v, 1917–18)

The detail of the legs, swollen and chafed by the chains, carries conviction; the description of the children is plainly intended to rouse pity. We are told that the enemies looking on are moved to tears and rebellious murmurs against the king by the spectacle; all this involves the reader in the situation and invokes his pity; words like 'veinqueur inhumain' (1909) and 'un Roy si felon' (1910) of Nabuchodonosor, 'pures victimes' (1912) of the children, imply a moral judgment on the action, even though in the context of the play the spectator may not be intended to accept this judgment without reservations. All the descriptions of cruelty and carnage in Garnier seem to be justified by their note of pity or indignation, and are relevant to what he is saying about war or the abuse of power. But in Montchrestien's description of, for example, the execution of Marie Stuart (in *L'Escossaise*) there is a kind of intimate horror, a playing on the reader's sensibilities by the mingling of the decorative and the repulsive, not linked to any theme of moral indignation:

> Un, deux, trois, quatre coups sur son col il delasche,
> Car le fer aceré moins cruel que son bras
> Vouloit d'un si beau corps differer le trespas.
> Le tronc tombe à la fin, et sa mourante face
> Par trois ou quatre fois bondit dessus la place.

(Act v)

Or, to take a passage which has a closer parallel in Garnier, consider Aman's threats against the Jews in Act i of Montchrestien's *Aman*:

> Non, puisque j'en vien là, je ne souffriray pas
> Que les enfans à naistre evitent le trespas:
> Qu'ils me soient arrachez du ventre de leurs meres,
> Et batus aux parois devant leurs propres peres,
> Afin qu'avec le jour l'espoir leur soit osté,
> De revivre jamais en leur postérité:
> Soient aux yeux des maris les femmes violées;
> Des Bourreaux impudents les Vierges soient soüillées,

133

Qu'on les estrangle apres d'un infame cordeau,
Ou qu'une pierre au col on les jette à vau-l'eau.
Bref que le sang fumeux ruisselle de la gorge
Des Hebrieux massacrez et ça et là regorge:
Que leurs corps tous relents n'ayent autres tombeaux,
Que les chiens affamez et les goulus corbeaux.

Compare this with the description of the execution of the prisoners at the end of *Les Juifves*, part of which is quoted on p. 132 above; one is a sad account of what has happened, the other an evil menace of what is to happen. We saw how Garnier's description carried an implied judgment of Nabuchodonosor's action. In the passage from *Aman*, on the other hand, words like 'Bourreaux impudents', 'infame cordeau' do not carry much weight of moral censure since they are spoken by the instigator of the massacre who is gloating over the bloody revenge he plans to take on the Jews; such words are part of a 'non-functional' rhetoric; they reinforce the impression of physical cruelty without conveying any attitude to that cruelty.

Another way of saying this is that in Garnier the emotional colour is kept in the right place. In the speech just quoted from *Aman*, the cruel words are being spoken by the wrong person. To hear the executioner describe the execution does not rouse pity so much as revulsion. Another example of such misplacing of the emotional colouring is in Montchrestien's *Les Lacènes*. In Act v, Ptolomée is about to kill Cléomène's mother and the rest of Cléomène's supporters, as an act of vengeance. He speaks to the dead friends whom he plans to avenge:

J'immole, chers amis, dessus vos froids tombeaux
Ces victimes, au lieu de vaches et d'agneaux;
Et si vous destournez le bel oeil de vostre ame
Sur mon esprit dolent que vostre perte entame,
Tous morts vous priserez mon immortel amour,
Qui parmi vostre cendre a choisi son sejour;
Mon coeur tout soupirant de mortelle souffrance,
Respire desormais cette seule esperance.

Ptolomée is the victor, he is about to kill his prisoners in cold blood. His speech is followed by one from the chorus on the bloodthirsty rage of an angry prince. One would expect any note of sadness, any hint of elegiac lament, to be kept for the prisoners. But in this speech, the mournful, defeated feeling seems to have spilled over into the victor's words. I think the reason for this apparent inconsistency is very simple. Garnier is a 'committed' artist, not to the extent of supporting a body of doctrine or partisan opinion, but in so far as he intends his plays to provoke some serious reflections on serious problems. Montchrestien has no such concern: his preoccupation is with language, which he handles with skill, producing effects of splendour, violence or gentle beauty. At any one moment in a Montchrestien play there is a distinct 'atmosphere': the characters are surrounded by an aura of quiet regret, of noble courage, of devoted love, or of some other readily definable emotion. But whether this 'atmosphere' is relevant to the theme of the play, or whether it has any logical relationship to the next 'atmosphere' which may abruptly replace it, between one speech and the next, seems to be of no importance. Garnier's *Leitmotiv* technique in *Hippolyte* is comparable, but he uses this to give each person in the play a distinct atmosphere of his or her own: Hippolyte's is the forest and hunting; Phèdre's is compounded of darkness, serpents and fire; Thésée's is Hades, and monsters. In Montchrestien the atmospheres blur rather than define the distinctions between the characters, as we saw in the example from *Les Lacènes*.

In Garnier, where there is emotional ambiguity it is appropriate: thus in *Porcie*, the conspirators are to be admired, pitied, mourned and blamed, and these different feelings are called upon in turn. In *Les Juifves* the emotional colouring is such as to make Nabuchodonosor alarming and Sédécie the object of compassion, even though the intellectual current of the play pulls us in the opposite direction, persuading us that Sédécie is wrong and Nabuchodonosor right: this dichotomy is very important as it helps to create the dimension of irony discussed in the previous chapter. Compare this with Montchrestien's *L'Escossaise* where Marie Stuart's 'constance' in the face of death is displayed for admiration without any complete examination of whether it is right or wrong for her to be executed. In Montchrestien this does not matter: in Garnier it would matter very much.

So far, I have been using comparison, to arrive at an idea of Garnier's technique by comparing it with that of other dramatists. We now come to two characteristics of his tragedies which in my opinion are unique, and which are of central importance in a study of his technique. An examination of them will show very clearly the highly individual nature of Garnier's political drama. I do not want to repeat here the comment on the political content of his work, which formed the matter of the middle chapters of this work, but to look at the way in which this content is incorporated into the tragedies. I am interested in two things: how the main political theme is worked into a play, and how the political element is 'orchestrated' with other modes of thought and feeling. I shall look at the plays in chronological order, beginning, therefore, with *Porcie*.

The presence of one dominating and unifying political theme does not exclude discussion of other political topics, and *Porcie* contains numerous political discussions on various subjects: in Act III alone, there are the *clémence/rigueur* debate, a statement of the necessity of peace, a soldiers' chorus discussing soldiers' wages, patriotic death and the fact that foreign war is preferable to civil. These are 'general' discussions, in the sense that they might be appropriate in another country or at another time. But they also fit into this particular play, where the main theme is tyrannicide and the chaos that follows it, and the central character is Rome itself, Rome torn by civil wars and threatened by a fresh tyranny to replace that which the conspirators destroyed. We are told in Act I that Rome must fall because she has been too great for too long; but there is no censure in the words Garnier uses to evoke this greatness ('généreux', 'magnanime', 'brave', 'puissance suprême'), for the greatness of Rome is admirable even if excessive. My suggestion that Rome is the central character in *Porcie* is borne out by the way in which the commonplaces in the play are made to centre on Rome or on Rome's political situation (i.e. the aftermath of tyrannicide, civil war), sometimes by being given a new twist. Here are some examples of this: in Act II (pp. 27–30), the chorus praises the life of retirement, or of country toil, as an escape not from worry or vice but from wars such as Rome is experiencing; in a long development of the commonplace theme of Fortune's mutability (Nourrice, Act I, pp. 30–32), Rome is taken as the exemplar; in Porcie's words on destiny (Act II, pp. 34–5) the vocabulary, with phrases such as 'sujet à leur force est le rond terrien' and 'l'entier gouvernement de la machine ronde', suggests a world-rule, a system such as Rome did in fact impose on a great part of the known world; when the chorus in Act III (pp. 51–3) rails against the injustice of Fortune, Garnier imitates a chorus in Seneca's *Hippolytus*—but adds 'tyran' to the list of wicked people favoured by Fortune.

The other important point is that the political and the personal are linked, with the political elements dominating the personal. Every personal feeling is slanted towards a political interest. Thus Porcie is proud of being Cato's daughter because he:

> Combatit ardemment pour nostre liberté.
> > (Act II, p. 26)

Comparing herself to Hecuba she says her misery is greater because of her political situation, with 'nos tyrans [. . .] prospérans', 'nos libertez vilement asservies' (Act II, p. 33). The argument between her and her nurse about whether she should die becomes a political discussion, the question under debate being whether her death would benefit the *patrie* (Act II, p. 34). In her great lamentation in Act IV (pp. 74–9), many of Porcie's words are devoted to historical and political facts, particularly those concerning the vicissitudes of Roman liberty. In the last act, the Chorus react to Porcie's death with a lament not so much for Porcie as for Rome (p. 82) and in their formal funeral hymn (led by the nurse) the themes are the City, Brute, and his blow for freedom; the nurse emphasizes that Porcie and Brute are fortunate to have escaped from the political disorder of Rome, and from the servitude endured by Romans (pp. 85–7).

Garnier's next play, *Hippolyte*, contains almost no political themes, and its 'orchestration' is of quite a different nature (see p. 135, above). But turning to Garnier's next political play, *Cornélie* (1574), we find once again that Rome occupies a central position in the play. The very long speech by Cicéron in the middle of the play (pp. 121–4; the speech is wrongly attributed to Cornélie in Pinvert's edition) is about Rome; there is much stress on the folly of Rome (Act IV, p. 134), her slavery (Act IV, p. 139), the mentality which leads to empire-building (Act I, pp. 100–1), the greatness of Rome (César's speech in Act IV, pp. 142–4, is a roll-call of the Roman world as well as an expression of the personal exultation of the world-ruler); the chorus at the end of Act II (pp. 115–17) describes how history repeats itself, by moving in cycles: this is applied to the history of Rome, and it would also give added point to Garnier's claim that this play is apt for his own country and century because it shows a 'grande République rompue par l'ambicieux discord de ses citoyens' (p. 90)—France is now threatened by the same danger that destroyed the Roman republic.

But Rome is not the only subject of the play; essentially, *Cornélie* is an interweaving of three themes, or rather, the interest shifts constantly between three modes or three levels of thought and feeling. In *Porcie* we noticed two such modes, the personal and the political, and we saw how the personal was always transformed into the political. In *Cornélie* the personal feeling is that aroused by the deaths of Pompée and Scipion (and by fearful anticipation of those deaths). The political interest centres on the threat to public and private liberty which is implicit in César's victory, and on the horror of war. The third level is philosophical, or 'humane' in the sense of dealing with the human condition. The play contains various combinations and interactions of these three fields of interest.

In Act II (pp. 105–6) we see the political subordinated to the personal when, with a disproportion worthy of Bossuet (who ascribes the English civil wars to God's plan for the salvation of Henriette Marie's soul), Cornélie claims that civil discord has been sent by the gods to punish her for remarrying after her first husband's death. The personal then enlarges into the philosophical as she moves from her own misery to a discourse on the human condition. A description of the life of the world as endless cycles of birth, death and rebirth leads to the theme of Roman history repeating itself: here the philosophical has shifted to the political.

In Act III (p. 124) a political speech (about Rome) is interrupted by a personal topic: the arrival of Philippes with Pompé's body, causing a renewal of personal grief.[1] From personal grief we move to a philosophical inquiry (p. 126): do the gods listen to prayer? is there divine justice? Then the political note returns (speech on ambition, p. 129); personal grief comes to the fore once again ('mes douleurs sont égales', p. 129), to be superseded by the political again, as Cornélie's speech defying César to hurt her contains not only a description of torture but a series of political accusations (p. 131).

In Act iv, César's address to Rome opens on a personal note, expressing his deep love of Rome almost tenderly (p. 142), in lines such as:

> O beau Tybre, et tes flots de grand'aise ronflans
> Ne doublent-ils leur crespe à tes verdureux flancs,
> Joyeux de ma venue?

Then as his 'jactance' develops, it is less a personal boast than a solemn listing of the Roman world (pp. 143–4)—one has this impression because of the many proper names given, and because César speaks of himself in the third person instead of continually emphasizing 'moi' as is common in the self-centred giants of Seneca's and Garnier's tragedies; his speech thus moves from the personal plane to the political.

In the last act comes Cornélie's supreme lament. Her grief is personal, but seems to leap to the philosophical plane by its large scale, its absoluteness (pp. 161–2). Her second and third speeches are political (pp. 162–3, 163–4), envisaging the future defeat and decay of Rome. Thus the three strains are combined and reconciled, in this last act, because they are all expressed by the same person.

I have given this fairly detailed analysis of *Porcie* and *Cornélie* because they are often dismissed as Garnier's weakest plays: looked at in terms of this pattern of different voices or

---

[1] Analysis in terms of an 'orchestration' effect offers an explanation of what is otherwise a weakness: we already knew that Pompé was dead, and Philippes's account of how he came by the body is confused; his appearance is meaningless except in terms of motivating a change from the political to the personal level of expression.

modes, they make sense and need no longer be regarded as a rather regrettable exercise in rhetoric.

Marc-Antoine receives less disdainful treatment from the critics than these two plays, but it too has had some hard words written about it. If the main character in *Porcie* and *Cornélie* is Rome, in *Marc-Antoine* this place is occupied by Love. Act I shows the degrading power of love: Marc-Antoine's political career has been ruined by it, and the final degradation is that he does not care. In Act II we are shown the other side—the ennobling power of love; we also see Diomède's ignoble view of how to use beauty, for selfish and political ends (p. 195). Act III returns to the tone of Act I, with further disillusionment and bitterness. Act IV represents a change in the angle from which the situation is observed: now we have the outsiders moralizing about the lovers; on the political level, we see those who have profited from this disastrous love and taken over political power; we also see some of their faults. The last Act is a consummation of suffering and grief, and the final expression of the pessimism in which the whole play is steeped, and which the chorus epitomized at the end of Act I (p. 177):

> Moindre estoit hier nostre ennuy
> Qu'ores, et demain sera pire
> Que n'est encores ce jourdhuy.

This brief summary is enough to indicate that in Act I at least, there is the same kind of interaction that we have already examined in *Porcie* and *Cornélie*. Some examples from other parts of the play will confirm that this play is organized on the same principles as the first two. In Act III we see a complete triumph of personal over political considerations in Marc-Antoine's speech:

> Ait César la victoire, ait mes biens, ait l'honneur
> D'estre sans compagnon de la terre seigneur;
> Ait mes enfans, ma vie au mal opiniâtre,
> Ce m'est tout un, pourveu qu'il n'ait ma Cléopâtre.
>
> (Act III, p. 201)

Indeed, the supreme personal consideration (love of Cléopâtre) triumphs also over less important personal considerations such as his own children ('Ait mes enfans').

In the same act, Marc-Antoine reminds us that in some people these values are reversed, by the force of political ambition (which he no longer feels):

> On permettra plustost aimer celle qu'on aime,
> Que de communiquer au sacré diadème.
> Toute chose on renverse et tout droit on esteint,
> Amitié, parentèle, et n'y a rien si saint
> Qu'on n'aille violant pour se rendre seul maistre:
> Et n'a-t-on soing comment, pourveu qu'on le puisse estre.
>
> (Act III, p. 204–5)

In the same long scene (which, with one chorus, forms the whole of Act III) comes another irruption of the personal, and of a fiercely individualistic viewpoint, this time into the safe world of the philosophical commonplace, when Marc-Antoine rejects the convenient scapegoat, Fortune, blamed by Lucile, and declares:

> Ce ne fut la Fortune à la face inconstante,
> Ce ne fut du Destin la force violente
> Qui forgea mon malheur. Hé! ne sçait-on pas bien
> Que c'est que l'un et l'autre, et qu'ils ne peuvent rien?
> Fortune que l'on craint, qu'on déteste et adore,
> N'est qu'un événement dont la cause on ignore.
> Encore bien souvent la cause on apperçoit,
> Mais l'effet se découvre autre qu'on ne pensoit.
>
> (Act III, p. 209)

In fact, he accepts full responsibility for his own life and for his own misfortune, as Cléopâtre does in Act II, in contradicting Charmion:

CHARMION: Telle estoit la rigueur de vostre destinée.
CLÉOPÂTRE: Telle estoit mon erreur et ma crainte obstinée.
CHARMION: Mais qu'y eussiés-vous fait s'il ne plaisoit aux dieus?
CLÉOPÂTRE: Les dieux sont tousjours bons, et non pernicieus.
CHARMION: N'ont-ils pas tout pouvoir sur les choses humaines?
CLÉOPÂTRE: Ils ne s'abaissent pas aux affaires mondaines,
    Ains laissent aux mortels disposer librement

De ce qui est mortel dessous le firmament.
Que si nous commettons en cela quelques fautes,
Il ne fault nous en prendre à leurs majestez hautes,
Mais à nous seulement, qui par nos passions
Journellement tombons en mille afflictions.

(Act ii, pp. 185–6)

Cléopâtre, like Marc-Antoine, is aware of her political destitution, but her personal grief overtops it:

Et ne portoy-je assez de cruelle misère,
Mon royaume perdant, perdant la liberté,
Ma tendre géniture, et la douce clairté
Du rayonnant soleil, et te perdant encore,
Antoine, mon souci, si je ne perdois ore
Ce qui me restoit plus? las! c'estoit ton amour,
Plus cher que sceptre, enfans, la liberté, le jour.

(Act ii, pp. 182–3)

Je pers de mes ayeux les sceptres anciens;
J'asservis ce royaume à des loix estrangères,
Et prive mes enfans des biens héréditaires.
Encore n'est-ce rien, las! ce n'est rien au prix
De vous, mon cher espous, par mes amorces pris,
De vous que j'infortune, et que de main sanglante
Je contrains dévaler sous la tombe relante,
De vous que je destruis, de vous, mon cher seigneur,
A qui j'oste la vie, et l'empire, et l'honneur.

(Act v, p. 231)

Octave represents a set of values exactly opposite to those of Marc-Antoine and Cléopâtre. His first reaction to the news of Marc-Antoine's death is personal regret and sympathy ('Je ne puis ne plorer' Act iv, p. 227) but his avarice (one of the characteristic qualities of the tyrant) soon reappears, and political greed completely stifles personal grief.

The difference between *Marc-Antoine* and the other two Roman plays is that here there is a conflict between personal and political values. Both the hero and heroine choose the personal, emotional value of their love for each other; this brings about their political ruin, which in turn leads to personal and emotional defeat as well. By choosing love they lose everything, including each other.

After *Porcie*, it seems as though Garnier decided to try a different kind of play, and he wrote the non-political *Hippolyte*, before returning to his own kind of political drama with *Cornélie* and *Marc-Antoine*. His next two plays represent a slight change of direction. Perhaps he was trying to remedy a lack of action and 'plot' in his earlier plays, for each of his next two tragedies (*La Troade* and *Antigone*) combines the substance of several Greek plays. In these two plays, instead of the shifting modes of feeling and thought which we have just seen in the Roman plays, the patterns are made by a group of political themes. In *La Troade* these are: the misery of war for both sides; the recurrent, inescapable memory of the brutal sack of Troy; the problem of the proper conduct of victor and vanquished; the bitter distress and humiliation of falling from royalty to miserable slavery. In *Antigone* the interwoven themes are: war and civil war, with their horrible aftermath; the lure of the crown; the king and the law; the conflict between moral duty and obedience to law. Act iv illustrates the method well, for the opening scene between Antigone and Ismène includes all these themes except that of the king and the law—which is supplied at the beginning of the next scene by Créon's first speech, ritually re-promulgating his edict.

With these two plays (*La Troade* and *Antigone*) there are moments when the plot seems a mere contrivance, a framework to which to fasten these various political themes. In *Les Juifves*, Garnier's last tragedy, the two elements are integrated, and we find again the movement between personal and political planes which is Garnier's most original contribution to political tragedy. The movement here is achieved by the presence of three great figures: Sédécie and Nabuchodonosor represent two poles of a political argument, while Amital, the Hecuba-figure, the innocent sufferer caught up in a quarrel which she tried to avert, bears the heaviest burden of personal involvement and grief.

Thus the political element in Garnier's tragedies is the

dominant strand in a harmonic pattern; a strand encompassing many themes, challenging to the intellect and worthy of special attention and analysis. The other two elements are less remarkable in content, however fine their expression: vast griefs and bitter humiliations dominate the personal element, while the philosophical consists mainly of commonplaces such as the mutability of Fortune and the value of the Golden Mean. But the political element contains serious reflections on contemporary problems; it leaves some questions unanswered; and it makes an impressive statement against war. Garnier has too often been compared pointlessly and irrelevantly to seventeenth-century dramatists. To find a similar compassion for the victims of war, one has to look back to Euripides's *Troades* or forward to Wilfred Owen's war-poems, insisting as painfully as Garnier's battle-scenes on the physical horrors of fighting, which cannot be eased by patriotic slogans:

> If you could hear, at every jolt, the blood
> Come gargling from the froth-corrupted lungs,
> Bitter as the cud
> Of vile, incurable sores on innocent tongues,—
> My friend, you would not tell with such high zest
> To children ardent for some desperate glory,
> The old lie: Dulce et decorum est
> Pro patria mori.

('Dulce et Decorum Est')

Owen is chiefly concerned with the suffering of the soldier in the field: but we have seen how often Garnier, like Euripides, directs our sympathy to those who endure the aftermath of war.

In the *œuvre* of many artists, particularly in the Renaissance, one characteristic figure or object may recur frequently enough to be recognized as the symbolic expression of a fundamental idea or preoccupation. Titian's concern with the passing of time is expressed by the frequent appearance in his portraits of the little Augsburg clock given him by Charles V. Velasquez's vision of the frailty and imperfection of humanity is epitomized by the dwarfs who people his courtly settings. Groups painted by Veronese often seem to be engaged in a symbolic encounter between youth and age or between rival cultures.

Garnier too has his characteristic image, the Mourning Woman.[1] Her grief may be for sons (Jocaste), a husband (Porcie, Cornélie), a lover (Cléopâtre, Phèdre) or a whole nation (Hécube, Amital); whichever of these she mourns, she is the most eloquent figure in Garnier's tragedy, and often voices his compassion and respect for the victims of war.

[1] The equivalent figure in Racine would be the woman in love, who seems to represent, for Racine, all the darkness and the glory of the human heart.

BIOGRAPHICAL APPENDIX

ALENÇON, FRANÇOIS DUC D' (1554–84)
Youngest surviving son of Henri II and Catherine de Médicis. In 1576 he acquired the title of Duc d'Anjou, which had been vacant since his elder brother became Henri III. Portraits show François as strikingly handsome, but in fact he was badly disfigured by confluent smallpox. He was ambitious and tried many paths to power, becoming suitor to Elizabeth I of England, leader of the 'Politiques' (the party of moderate Protestants and malcontent Catholics), ally of Henri de Navarre and would-be 'liberator' of the Netherlands. His early death (of tuberculosis) was probably a relief to his harassed brother Henri III.

ANJOU, DUC D'. See ALENÇON, FRANÇOIS DUC D', and HENRI III

BOURBON, ANTOINE DE (1518–62)
Duc de Vendôme, he became King of Navarre in 1555 by his marriage to Jeanne III d'Albret. He was a Protestant leader at the beginning of the civil wars, but soon abandoned the Protestant cause, thinking that friendship with Philip II might enable him to increase his little kingdom by regaining the part of it south of the Pyrenees, seized by Spain in 1511.

BOURBON, HENRI DE (1553–1610)
Son of Antoine de Bourbon, he became King of Navarre in 1572, at the death of his mother, Jeanne III d'Albret. In the same year he married Marguerite de Valois (daughter of Henri II); the marriage was later dissolved. A leader of the Protestant cause, he escaped the St. Bartholomew massacre by abjuring, but soon resumed his command of the Protestant forces. He was named by Henri III as his legitimate successor and became king (as Henri IV) in 1589, although he could not take full possession of his kingdom until he had finally crushed the Ligue, and abjured Protestantism again. He was assassinated in 1610.

CHARLES IX (1550–74)
The second of Henri II's sons to become king, he succeeded his brother, François II, in 1560; his mother, Catherine de Médicis, was his

Regent until 1563, and continued to exercise great influence on him for most of his reign. He was a violent, unbalanced character whose amusements were hunting, and making armour on a forge which he had installed in the Louvre. In 1571–2 he came under the influence of Coligny, to an extent which alarmed his Catholic advisers, including his mother, whose eagerness to regain control over him probably led to the Massacre of Saint Bartholomew. For this Massacre, Charles IX must bear responsibility, even though it was executed, and probably planned, by others.

COLIGNY, GASPARD DE (1519–72)
Thanks to his relationship to the powerful house of Montmorency, Gaspard was named Colonel-Général de l'Infanterie (by Henri II) at the age of twenty-six. He relinquished the charge to his younger brother D'Andelot, in order to become Amiral de France. A convert to Protestantism, he became one of the outstanding French Protestant leaders, and one of the most honourable and praiseworthy on either side. His influence over Charles IX (whom he tried to interest in a war against Spain in the Netherlands) led to the Guise attempt to assassinate Coligny, and, perhaps, to the St. Bartholomew massacre of which he was the first victim.

CONDÉ, LOUIS Ier DE BOURBON, PRINCE DE (1530–69)
'Le petit homme' led the Protestants in the early years of the religious wars, till he was defeated by Henri, duc d'Anjou (later Henri III) at Jarnac. He had already surrendered when he was killed by the Captain of the Duc d'Anjou's guard; some suppose that this was done on the Duc d'Anjou's orders, but it seems unlikely.

CONDÉ, HENRI Ier DE BOURBON, PRINCE DE (1552–88)
Son of the above. A young man when his father died, Henri assumed his responsibilities as one of the leaders of the Protestants, and he and Henri de Navarre were the two most prominent Protestant princes. Like Henri, he escaped the St. Bartholomew by a temporary abjuration of his religion. He married, in 1572, Marie de Clèves with whom Henri III (then Duc d'Anjou) was probably in love.

GARNIER, ROBERT (1545–90)
Born in La Ferté-Bernard (in the modern department of Sarthe); studied law at Toulouse, where he was a prize-winner in the poetry competition of the Jeux Floraux. After a short stay in Paris, he returned

to his own part of the country and became a magistrate in Le Mans, being promoted to Lieutenant criminel in 1574. His plays were published in the period 1568–83. In 1587 he became a member of the Grand Conseil, a sort of peripatetic High Court, appointed by the king. He was also, for a brief period at the end of his life, a member of the Ligue. Although writing was never his full-time profession, it was a disappointment to him that his plays were not performed at Court.

GUISE, FRANÇOIS DE LORRAINE, DUC DE (1519–63)
The Guise family became powerful at the death of Henri II, when their niece, Marie Stuart, was Queen of France. François, known as Le Balafré from a conspicuous scar on his face, already had a great reputation as a soldier before he took command of the Catholic troops at the beginning of the wars of religion. (With his brother Charles, Cardinal de Lorraine, he was partly responsible for the outbreak of these wars by his part in the massacre of Wassy or Vassy, 1562). He was shot by a Protestant, Poltrot de Méré, at Orléans.

GUISE, HENRI Ier, DUC DE (1550–88)
Elder son of the above. Only a boy when his father was killed, Henri inherited his popularity and became in his turn a leader of the Catholics. In the third civil war he fought at Jarnac and Moncontour, and acquired a scar which enabled him to inherit also his father's nickname of Le Balafré. He was one of the instigators of a plot to kill Coligny, and probably of the Massacre of St. Bartholomew a few days after the failure of the assassination attempt. As a leader of the Ligue, he almost overthrew Henri III, and came closest to doing so on the Journée des Barricades (May, 1588) after a triumphal entry into Paris. He failed to seize his opportunity and Henri III had him killed at Blois a few months later (December, 1588).

HENRI III (1551–89)
The last of the Valois kings and the third son of Henri II to come to the throne. Christened Alexandre Edouard, and given the title of Duc d'Angoulême, his name was changed to Henri in 1566 when he received the duchy of Anjou as his apanage. As Duc d'Anjou he was made Lieutenant général, commanded the royal troops in the third civil war and was acclaimed for his victories at Jarnac and Moncontour (1569). He was never to enjoy such popularity again. His share of responsibility in the Massacre of Saint Bartholomew is uncertain.

In 1573 he was elected King of Poland; in 1574, when news reached him of the death of Charles IX, he left Poland hurriedly to claim the French throne. He was an intelligent ruler but the odds against him were too heavy. He was never able to pacify his troubled kingdom, and matters were exacerbated by his failure to produce an heir. The ultra-Catholic Ligue, led by the Guise family, became more and more menacing, until Henri was driven to order the murder of the Duc de Guise and his brother the Cardinal. Henri then made peace with the Protestants, led by Henri de Navarre; but before he could profit from this new disposition of forces, he was assassinated by a monk, Jacques Clément. Before dying he had time to insist on Henri de Navarre's recognition as his legitimate heir.

L'HOSPITAL, MICHEL DE (1505–73)

As Chancelier de France from 1560, he tried to prevent, and then put a stop to, the wars of religion, and was responsible for a number of edicts of tolerance. In 1568 he refused to fix the Great Seal to an edict forbidding the Protestants to hold services, and ordering their ministers to leave the country within two weeks. He was forced to retire from public office, leaving the government in the hands of the ultra-Catholics led by the Cardinal de Lorraine (brother of François, duc de Guise). His liberal and tolerant views found expression in a number of speeches and 'Discours'.

MAYENNE, CHARLES DE LORRAINE, DUC DE (1554–1611)

Younger brother of Henri de Guise, he was one of the commanders of the Ligue's forces. After the death of Henri de Guise, Mayenne entered Paris, was named Lieutenant général and assumed complete command of the Ligue. He led the resistance to Henri IV, but was defeated at Ivry and surrendered in 1595.

MÉDICIS, CATHERINE DE (1519–89)

Wife of Henri II, she was Queen for twelve years, Queen Mother for thirty (during the reigns of François II, Charles IX and Henri III). Officially, she was Regent only during the brief minority of Charles IX, but was politically active during the reigns of all her three sons. Her object was always to achieve a balance of power between the rival factions, and her mistake was to underestimate the strength of the feelings on which those factions were based, whether religious zeal or personal animosity. She was shrewd, ingenious and tireless in the execution of her plans; but her youngest, and favourite, son Henri III preferred to trust his own judgment and tried (not always successfully) to prevent her intervention in affairs of state.

PIBRAC, GUY DU FAUR DE (1529–86)
Noted both as a magistrate and a man of letters, Pibrac was one of Henri III's trusted advisers. He accompanied him to Poland, and later tried to negotiate with the Poles to keep Henri as their king, in spite of his accession to the French throne. His *Quatrains*, typical of the period in their blend of Christianity and Stoicism, were widely read and often reprinted.

BIBLIOGRAPHY

I. SIXTEENTH-CENTURY PLAYS, WORKS ON DRAMATIC
THEORY, ETC.

BUCHANAN, GEORGE. *Baptistes, sive Calumnia*. London, 1577.

—— *Jephthes, sive Votum*. Paris, 1554.

—— *Jephté* (Florent Chrestien's translation of *Jephthes, sive Votum*). Paris, 1567.

CHANTELOUVE, FRANÇOIS DE. *La Tragedie de feu Gaspar de Colligni jadis Admiral de France, contenent ce qui advint à Paris le 24 Aoust 1572, avec le nom des personnages. s.l.*, 1575.

CISSÉ, JACQUES DE COURTIN DE. *Hymnes de Synese traduits de grec en françois*. Paris, 1581.

DESMASURES, LOUIS. *Tragédies saintes*, ed. Charles Comte. Paris, 1907.

DORAT, JEAN. *J. Aurati . . . poemata*. Paris, 1586.

FILLEUL, NICHOLAS. *Achille, tragédie françoise en cinq actes, en vers*. Paris, 1563.

—— *La Lucrèce*, in: *Les Théâtres de Gaillon à la Reine*. Rouen, 1873 (facsimile of 1566 edition).

FONTENY, JACQUES DE. *Cléophon, tragédie conforme et semblable à celles que la France a veues durant les guerres civilles*. Paris, 1600.

GARNIER, ROBERT.

Early editions

—— *Porcie, tragedie françoise, representant la cruelle et sanglante saison des guerres civiles de Rome. Propre et convenable pour y voir depeincte la calamité de ce temps*. Paris, 1568.

—— *Hippolyte, tragedie*. Paris, 1573.

—— *Cornelie, tragedie*. Paris, 1574.

—— *Marc Antoine, tragedie*. Paris, 1578.

—— *La Troade, tragedie*. Paris, 1579.

—— *Antigone ou la pieté, tragedie*. Paris, 1580.

—— *Bradamante, tragecomedie*. Paris, 1582.

—— *Les Juifves, tragedie*. Paris, 1583.

—— *Les tragedies de R.G.* Paris, 1585.

Modern editions used for this work

—— *Œuvres complètes (théâtre et poésies)*, ed. Lucien Pinvert. Paris, 1923. Vol. I (*Porcie, Cornélie, Marc-Antoine, Hippolyte*).

—— *Œuvres complètes: Les Juifves, Bradamante, Poésies diverses*, ed. Raymond Lebègue. Paris, 1949.

—— *Œuvres complètes: La Troade, Antigone*, ed. Raymond Lebègue. Paris, 1952.

GRÉVIN, JACQUES. *Théâtre complet et poésies choisies*, ed. Lucien Pinvert. Paris, 1922.

GUERSENS, CAYE JULE DE. *Panthee, tragedie, prise du grec de Xenophon*. Poitiers, 1571.

JODELLE, ESTIENNE. *Les Œuvres et meslanges poetiques d'Estienne Jodelle sieur du Lymodin*, ed. C. Marty-Laveaux. 2 vols. Paris, 1868–70.

LA PERUSE, JEAN BASTIER DE. *La Medee, tragedie. Et autres diverses poesies*. Poitiers, *s.d.* (1555?).

LA TAILLE, JEAN DE. *De l'Art de la tragédie*, ed. F. West. Manchester, 1939.

—— *La Famine, ou les Gabeonites, tragedie prise de la Bible, et suivant celle de Saül. Ensemble plusieurs autres œuvres poëtiques*. Paris, 1573 (contains *Alexandre* and *Daire*, the two tragedies by Jean de la Taille's brother Jacques).

—— *Saül le furieux*, in *Münchener Beiträge zur romanischen und englischen Philologie*, XL, 1908. (See entry under A. Werner in part III of this bibliography.)

LE BRETON, GABRIEL. *Adonis*. Rouen, 1599.

MARLOWE, CHRISTOPHER. *Works*, ed. R. H. Case. 6 vols. London, 1931–4.

MATTHIEU, PIERRE. *La Guisiade*. Lyon, 1589.

MIRANDULA, OCTAVIANUS. *Illustrium poëtarum flores, per Octavianum Mirandulam collecti, et in locos communes digesti*. Lyon, 1553.

MONTCHRESTIEN, ANTOINE DE. *Aman*, ed. G. O. Seiver. Philadelphia and London, 1939.

—— *Les Tragédies*, ed. L. Petit de Julleville (*Bibliothèque Elzévirienne*). Paris, 1891.

MURET, MARC-ANTOINE DE. *Opera omnia*. 4 vols. Leyden, 1789.

RIVAUDEAU, ANDRÉ DE. *Les Œuvres poétiques d'André de Rivaudeau gentilhomme de Bas Poitou*, ed. C. Mourain de Sourdeval. Paris, 1859.

ROILLET, CLAUDE. *Varia poemata*. Paris, 1556.

RONSARD, PIERRE DE. *Œuvres complètes*, ed. P. Laumonier. Paris, 1914–67.

Saint Gelais, Mellin de. *Œuvres complètes,* ed. Prosper Blanchemain. Paris, 1873.

Scaliger, Julius Caesar. *Poetices libri septem.* Lyon, 1561.

Seneca, Lucius Annaeus. *Tragedies.* 2 vols. London (Loeb Classical Library), 1917.

Toutain, Charles. *La Tragedie d'Agamemnon, avec deus livres de chants de philosophie et d'amour.* Paris, 1557.

II. POLITICAL THEORY AND PROPAGANDA

Advertissement sur le pourparlé, qu'on dit de paix, entre le Roy et ses rebelles. Avec son contrepoison. Paris, 1568.

Albon, Claude d'. *De la Majesté royalle, institution et preeminence, et des faveurs divines particulieres envers icelle.* Lyon, 1575.

Aurigny, Gilles d'. *Le Livre de police humaine.* Paris, 1544.

Baïf, Jean Antoine de. *Epistre au Roy, sous le nom de la Royne sa mere: pour l'instruction d'un bon roy.* Paris, 1575.

Barnaud, Nicolas (?). *Le Cabinet du Roy de France, dans lequel il y a trois perles precieuses d'inestimable valeur. s.l.,* 1581.

—— (?) *Le Miroir des Francois, compris en trois livres. s.l.,* 1581.

—— (?) *Le Reveille-matin des Francois et de leurs voisins.* 'Edimbourg', 1574.

Belleforest, François de. *Arraisonnement fort gentil et proffitable sur l'infelicité qui suyt ordinairement le bonheur des grans.* Paris, 1569.

Belleforest, François de. *Les Grandes annales, et histoire generale de France, des la venue des Francs en Gaule, jusques au regne du roy tres-Chrestien Henry III.* 2 vols. Paris, 1579.

Bèze, Théodore de. *De l'Authorité du magistrat en la punition des heretiques, et du moyen d'y proceder.* Geneva, 1560.

—— *Du Droit des magistrats sur leurs subiets. s.l.,* 1574.

Bodin, Jean. *Les Six livres de la republique.* Paris, 1576.

Budé, Guillaume. *Le Livre de l'institution du prince,* ed. Jean de Luxembourg. Paris, 1547.

Calvin, Jean. *L'Institution chrétienne.* Geneva, 1560.

—— *Lettres de Jean Calvin,* ed. Jules Bonnet. 2 vols. Paris, 1854.

Champier, Symphorien. *La Nef des princes et des batailles de noblesse avec aultres enseignemens utilz et profitables.* Lyon, 1502.

Desautelz, Guillaume. *Harengue au peuple francois contre la rebellion.* Paris, 1560.

Du Belloy, Pierre. *Apologie catholique. s.l.,* 1585.

DU HAILLAN, BERNARD DE GIRARD. *De l'Estat et succez des affaires de France.* Paris, 1570.

DU TILLET, JEAN. *Les Memoires et recerches.* Rouen, 1578.

ESPENCE, CLAUDE D'. *L'Institution d'un prince chrestien.* Paris, 1548.

GENTILLET, INNOCENT. *Discours, sur les moyens de bien gouverner et maintenir en bonne paix un Royaume ou autre Principauté. Contre Nicolas Machiavel Florentin.* s.l., 1576.

—— *Remonstrance au Roy treschrestien Henry III de ce nom, Roy de France et de Pologne.* Frankfurt, 1574.

GOUSTÉ, CLAUDE. *Traicté de la puissance et authorité des roys.* s.l., 1561.

GRASSAILLE, CHARLES DE. *Regalium Franciae.* . . . Lyon, 1538.

HENRI III. *Harangue faite par le roy estant en son conseil le 16 juin à la publication de 26 edicts.* Paris, 1586.

HOTMAN, FRANÇOIS. *Franco-Gallia.* Geneva, 1573.

LA MADELEYNE, JEAN DE. *Discours de l'estat et office d'un bon roy, prince ou monarque, pour bien et heureusement regner sur la terre, et pour garder et maintenir ses subjectz en paix, union et obeissance.* Paris, 1575.

LA TAILLE, JEAN DE. *Le Prince nécessaire,* in *Oeuvres,* ed. René de Maulde. 4 vols. Paris, 1882, vol IV.

LE ROY, LOUIS. *Consideration sur l'histoire françoise, et l'universelle de ce temps, dont les merveilles sont succinctement recitees.* Paris, 1567.

—— *Des Differens et troubles advenans entre les hommes par la diversité des opinions en la religion.* Paris, 1562. 2nd. ed., 1563.

—— *De l'Excellence du gouvernement royal.* Paris, 1575.

—— *Exhortation aux Francois pour vivre en concorde, et jouir du bien de la paix.* Paris, 1570.

—— *Les Monarchiques.* (Outline of unwritten book, printed as appendix to *Exhortation.*)

—— *De l'Origine, antiquité, progres, excellence et utilité de l'art politique.* Paris, 1567.

—— *Trois livres d'Isocrates ancien orateur et philosophe.* Paris, 1551.

—— *De la Vicissitude ou varieté des choses en l'univers.* Paris, 1579.

L'HOSPITAL, MICHEL DE. *Discours sur la pacification des troubles de l'an M.D. LXVII.* s.l., 1568.

—— *Œuvres,* ed. P. J. S. Dufey. 5 vols. Paris, 1824–5.

MACHIAVELLI, NICCOLO. *Discorsi sopra la Prima Deca de T. Livio.* Florence, 1531.

—— *Il Principe,* ed. L. A. Burd. Oxford, 1891.

—— *The Prince,* trans. George Bull. Harmondsworth, 1961.

Mémoires de Condé. London and Paris, 1743.

Mémoires de l'Estat de France, sous Charles neufiesme. 3 vols. Meidelbourg, 1577.

Mémoires de la Ligue, contenant les évenemens les plus remarquables depuis 1576, jusqu'à la Paix accordée entre le Roi de France et le Roi d'Espagne, en 1598. 6 vols. Amsterdam, 1758.

PASQUIER, ETIENNE. *Le Pourparler du prince*, first published in 1560. Reprinted in *Les Recherches de la France*. Paris, 1660.

PIBRAC, GUY DU FAUR DE. *Harangue ou remonstrance derniere prononcee à la Cour*. (1562). Paris, 1603.

—— *Les Quatrains*. Paris, 1576. 2nd edition Lyon, 1597.

SAINT THOMAS, FRANÇOIS DE. *La Vraye forme de bien et heureusement regir, et gouverner un royaume ou Monarchie: ensemble le vray office d'un bon Prince*. Lyon, 1569.

SEYSSEL, CLAUDE DE. *La Grand' Monarchie de France*. Paris, 1557. (1st edition 1519.)

—— *La Monarchie de France*, ed. Jacques Poujol. (Modern, critical edition of above.) Paris, 1961.

SORBIN, ARNAULT. *Le Vray Resveille-matin des calvinistes, et republicains françois*. Paris, 1576.

—— (ed.) *Le Vray discours des derniers propos memorables, et trespas du feu Roy de tres bonne memoire Charles neufiesme*. Paris, 1574.

SPIFAME, RAOUL. *Dicaearchiae Henrici regis Christianissimi progymnasmata. s.l.n.d.* (1556?)

THILLARD, JEAN HELUÏS DE. *Le Miroüer du prince chretien*. Paris, 1566.

Le Tombeau du feu Roy Tres Chrestien Charles IX. Paris, 1574.

III. HISTORICAL AND CRITICAL WORKS, ETC.

AITKEN, J. M. *The trial of George Buchanan before the Lisbon Inquisition*. Edinburgh, 1939.

ALLEN, J. W. *A history of political thought in the sixteenth century*. London, 1928.

ARMSTRONG, W. A. 'The Elizabethan conception of the Tyrant', in *R.E.S.*, vol. XXII, 1946.

—— 'The influence of Seneca and Machiavelli on the Elizabethan Tyrant', in *R.E.S.*, vol. XXIV, 1948.

BARBIER, PIERRE. *Le Théâtre militant au seizième siècle*. Bourg, 1872.

BARRÈRE, JOSEPH. 'Observations sur quelques ouvrages politiques anonymes du seizième siècle', in *R.H.L.F.*, 21, 1914.

BAUDIN, MAURICE. ' "L'Art de régner" in seventeenth-century French tragedy', in *M.L.N.*, 50, 1935.

—— 'The shifting of responsibility in seventeenth-century French tragic drama', in *M.L.N.*, 49, 1934.

BERNAGE, M. S. *Etude sur Robert Garnier*. Paris, 1880.

BEVER, JEAN. 'Un Précurseur méconnu de notre théâtre classique: Robert Garnier (1545–1601)' (*sic*) in *Revue de France*, 6, 1925.

BÖHM, KARL. *Beiträge zur Kenntnis des Einflusses Seneca's auf die in der Zeit von 1552 bis 1562 erschienenen französischen Tragödien. Münchener Beiträge zur romanischen u. englischen Philologie*, XXIV, 1902.

BRADBROOK, M. C. *Themes and conventions of Elizabethan tragedy*. Cambridge, 1935. 2nd edition, 1960.

BUSH, DOUGLAS. *Classical influences in Renaissance literature*. Martin Classical Lectures, 23. Cambridge, Mass., 1952.

BUTLER, PHILIP. *Classicisme et Baroque dans l'œuvre de Racine*. Paris, 1959.

CARDASCIA, G. 'Machiavel et Jean Bodin', in *B.H.R.*, 3, 1943.

CHARBONNIER, F. *La Poésie française et les guerres de religion (1560–1574)*. Paris, 1919.

CHARDON, HENRI. *Robert Garnier: sa vie, ses poésies inédites avec son véritable portrait et un fac-simile de sa signature*. Paris and Le Mans, 1905.

CHARLTON, H. B. *The Senecan tradition in Renaissance tragedy*. Manchester, 1946 (first published 1921).

CHÉREL, ALBERT. *La Pensée de Machiavel en France*. Paris, 1935.

CHURCH, WILLIAM FARR. *Constitutional thought in sixteenth-century France. A study in the evolution of ideas*. Harvard Historical Studies, 47. Cambridge, Mass., 1941.

DALEY, T. A. *Jean de la Taille (1533–1608). Etude historique et littéraire*. Paris, 1934.

ELLIS-FERMOR, UNA. *The Jacobean drama, an interpretation*. London, 1953.

ENGLAND, SYLVIA LENNIE. *The Massacre of Saint Bartholomew*. London, 1938.

ERLANGER, PHILIPPE. *Henri III*. Paris, 1948. (11th edition.)

FAGUET, EMILE. *La Tragédie française au seizième siècle (1550–1600)*. Paris, 1883.

FRICK, DORA. *Robert Garnier als barocker Dichter*. Zürich, 1951.

GIRAULT, CHARLES. *La Famille de Robert Garnier*. Le Mans, 1935.

GOURCUFF, OLIVIER DE. *Un Ami de Ronsard. Robert Garnier.* Limoges, 1924.

GRAS, MAURICE. *Robert Garnier. Son art et sa méthode.* (Travaux d'Humanisme et Renaissance, LXXII) Geneva, 1965.

GRIFFITHS, RICHARD M. *The dramatic technique of Montchrestien.* (Ph.D. thesis, University of Cambridge, 1961.)

—— 'Les Sentences et le "but moral" dans les tragédies de Montchrestien', in *R.S.H.*, 105, 1962.

GUNDERSHEIMER, W. L. *The life and works of Louis Le Roy.* Geneva, 1966.

HAAG, EUGÈNE ET EMILE. *La France Protestante.* 10 vols. Paris and Geneva, 1846–59.

—— *La France Protestante,* 2nd edition, ed. Henri Bordier. 6 vols. (incomplete). Paris, 1877–88.

HARASZTI, JULES. 'La Littérature dramatique au temps de la Renaissance considérée dans ses rapports avec la scène contemporaine', *compte-rendu* in *R.H.L.F.*, XI, 1904.

HOLL, FRITZ. *Das politische und religiöse Tendenzdrama des XVI. Jahrhunderts in Frankreich. Münchener Beiträge zur romanischen u. englischen Philologie,* XXVI, 1903.

JENKINS, HOWELL. *Les Bienséances dans la tragédie française de la Renaissance.* (Thesis for Doctorat de l'Université de Paris, 1957.)

KAHNT, PAUL. *Der Gedankenkreis der Sentenzen in Jodelle's und Garnier's Tragödien und Seneca's Einfluss auf denselben.* Marburg, 1887.

KINGDON, R. M. 'Les Idées politiques de Bèze d'après son "Traitté de l'authorité du magistrat" ', in *B.H.R.*, XXII, 1960.

KÖRNER, PAUL. *Der Versbau Robert Garniers.* Berlin, 1894.

LA FORCE, M. LE DUC DE. *Inauguration d'un buste de Robert Garnier, à la Ferté-Bernard (16 septembre 1934).* Paris, 1934.

LANCASTER, H. CARRINGTON. 'The Rule of Three Actors in French Sixteenth Century Tragedy', in *M.L.N.*, 23, 1908.

LANSON, GUSTAVE. *Esquisse d'une histoire de la tragédie française.* New York, 1920. 2nd edition, Paris, 1954.

LAWTON, H. W. *Handbook of French Renaissance Dramatic Theory.* Manchester, 1949.

LEBÈGUE, RAYMOND. *Robert Garnier. Les Juifves.* Paris (*cours polycopié*), 1944–5.

—— 'Notes sur la tragédie française', in *B.H.R.*, 9, 1947.

—— 'Le Répertoire d'une troupe française à la fin du XVIe siècle', in *Revue de l'Histoire du Thèatre*, 1948.

——— 'Les Représentations dramatiques à la Cour des Valois', in *Fêtes de la Renaissance*, ed. J. Jacquot, Paris, 1956.

——— 'La Représentation des tragédies au XVIe siècle', in *Mélanges Chamard*, ed. R. L. Graeme Ritchie, Cambridge, 1951.

——— 'Tableau de la tragédie française de 1573 à 1610', in *B.H.R.*, 5, 1944.

——— *La Tragédie religieuse en France* (*1514–73*). Paris, 1929.

——— *La Tragédie française de la Renaissance*. Brussels, 1944.

LENIENT, C. *La Satire en France, ou la littérature militante au seizième siècle*. Paris, 1866.

LOUKOVITCH, KOSTA. *La Tragédie religieuse classique en France*. Paris, 1933.

LUCAS, F. L. *Seneca and Elizabethan tragedy.* Cambridge, 1922.

MARIÉJOL, J. H. *La Réforme et la Ligue*. Paris, 1904. (Vol. VI, part 1 of *Histoire de France depuis les origines jusqu'à la Révolution*, ed. Ernest Lavisse.)

MATTHIEU, PIERRE. *Histoire des derniers troubles de France*. 4 parts. *s.l.*, 1600. (1st edition Lyon, 1594–5.)

MAULNIER, THIERRY. *Introduction à la poésie française*. Paris, 1939.

MERCIER, CHARLES. 'Les Théories politiques des Calvinistes en France au cours des guerres de religion', in *Bulletin de la Société de l'Histoire Protestante*, 83, 1934.

MESNARD, PIERRE. *L'Essor de la philosophie politique au XVIe siècle*. Paris, 1936.

MEYER, EDWARD. *Machiavelli and the Elizabethan drama*. Weimar, 1897.

MOUFLARD, MARIE-MADELEINE. *Robert Garnier* (*1545–90*). *Etude biographique et littéraire*. (Thesis for Doctorat d'Etat. 10 vols. 1957.)

——— *Robert Garnier* (*1545–90*). *La Vie*. La Ferté-Bernard, 1961.

——— *Robert Garnier* (*1545–90*). *L'Œuvre*. La Roche-sur-Yon, 1963.

——— *Robert Garnier* (*1545–90*). *Les Sources*. La Roche-sur-Yon, 1964.

MYSING, OSKAR. *Robert Garnier und die antike Tragödie*. Leipzig, 1891.

NOGUÈRES, HENRI. *La Saint Barthélemy*. Paris, 1959.

OWEN, WILFRED. *Poems*, ed. Edmund Blunden, London, 1933.

PRAZ, MARIO. *The Flaming Heart*. New York, 1958.

PURKIS, HELEN MARY. *Les Ecrits théoriques sur le théâtre en France au XVIe siècle*. (Thesis for Doctorat de l'Université de Paris, 1952.)

REUTER, OTTO. *Der Chor in der französischen Tragödie. Romanische Studien, VI.* Berlin, 1904.

REYNOLDS, BEATRICE. *Proponents of limited monarchy in sixteenth-century France. Francis Hotman and Jean Bodin.* New York, 1931.

RIGAL, E. 'La Mise en scène dans les tragédies du XVIe siècle', in *R.H.L.F.*, XII, 1905.

ROATEN, DARNELL. *Structural forms in the French theater, 1500–1700.* Philadelphia, 1960.

ROLLAND, JOACHIM. *La Tragédie française au seizième siècle: 'Les Juifves'.* Paris, 1911.

ROMIER, LUCIEN. *Le Royaume de Catherine de Médicis.* Paris, 1925.

—— *La Conjuration d'Amboise.* Paris, 1932.

—— *Catholiques et Huguenots à la Cour de Charles IX.* Paris, 1924.

SAULNIER, V.-L. 'Un Ami inconnu de Robert Garnier, le poète Estienne Gasteuil', in *Revue universitaire*, vol. LXI, 1952.

—— 'Etienne Gasteuil, apologiste de Robert Garnier', in *Bulletin du Bibliophile et du bibliothécaire*, 3, 1959.

SEARLES, COLBERT. 'The stageability of Garnier's tragedies', in *M.L.N.*, 22, 1907.

SEGUIN, JEAN PIERRE. *L'Information en France de Louis XII à Henri II.* (Travaux d'Humanisme et Renaissance, XLIV.) Geneva, 1961.

THOMPSON, J. W. *The Wars of Religion in France, 1559–76.* Chicago, 1909.

WAILLE, VICTOR. *Machiavel en France.* Paris, 1884.

WEILL, G. *Les Théories sur le pouvoir royal en France pendant les guerres de religion.* Paris, 1891.

WERNER, A. *Jean de la Taille und sein 'Saül le furieux'. Münchener Beiträge zur romanischen u. englischen Philologie*, XL, 1908. (Includes text of Saül.)

WILLNER, KURT. *Montchrestiens Tragödien und die stoische Lebensweisheit.* Berlin, 1932.

YATES, FRANCES A. 'Some new light on *L'Ecossaise* of Antoine de Montchrestien', in *M.L.R.*, XXII, 1927.

ZANTA, L. *La Renaissance du stoïcisme au seizième siècle.* Paris, 1914.

INDEX

For the plays of Garnier and Seneca, the index includes references only to those passages where a play is either quoted, or discussed in some detail.